DIGITAL TRUST

Social Media Strategies to
Increase Trust and Engage Customers

BARRY CONNOLLY

BLOOMSBURY BUSINESS
LONDON · OXFORD · NEW YORK · NEW DELHI · SYDNEY

BLOOMSBURY BUSINESS
Bloomsbury Publishing Plc
50 Bedford Square, London, WC1B 3DP, UK

BLOOMSBURY, BLOOMSBURY BUSINESS and the Diana logo are
trademarks of Bloomsbury Publishing Plc

First published in Great Britain 2020

A catalogue record for this book is available from the British Library

Library of Congress Cataloguing-in-Publication data has been applied for

ISBN: 978-1-4729-6134-1; eBook: 978-1-4729-6135-8

2 4 6 8 10 9 7 5 3 1

Typeset by Deanta Global Publishing Services, Chennai, India
Printed and bound in Great Britain by CPI Group (UK) Ltd, Croydon CR0 4YY

To find out more about our authors and books visit www.bloomsbury.com
and sign up for our newsletters

33614082023796

CONTENTS

LIST OF TABLES AND FIGURES

List of Tables

List of Figures

Introduction

How do brands build trust and engage with customers? This question is at the forefront of every organization's strategic thinking, no matter whether they are a long-established company or a fledgling start-up. Digital technologies have not only created new social networks but also dramatically altered how consumer trust is formed with brands. Trust is a concept that has been analysed alongside many different disciplines over the years, such as philosophy, economics, sociology and management. Within marketing research in particular there have also been numerous academic studies that have investigated trust.

Trust can take years to earn and only a matter of seconds to lose, so it's important to keep trust at the forefront of everything that brands do, especially those brands who are active on social media. Indeed, no matter how well a business manages to build consumer trust, one error can cause the whole relationship to fall apart. The development of social media platforms such as Facebook, Twitter and Instagram have provided brands with a wealth of new opportunities to engage with their existing and prospective customers. Here are some quick-fire stats to highlight social media's importance to brands, as provided by Statistica.com (2018).

- About 92 per cent of B2B marketers in North America use social media content as part of their marketing tactics;
- Small and medium-sized enterprise (SME) owners also use social media as a marketing tool, as 68 per cent of American SMEs have stated having a profile on social networking sites;

- About 58.6 per cent of American consumers interact with brands on social media around one to three times per day;
- The brand's social media account is the preferred online channel of 40 per cent of women in the United States.

In the United States in particular, Facebook, Instagram and Twitter are considered the best social media platforms for engaging with consumers. Due to their ubiquity and substantial reach, social media brand communities (SMBCs) have proven to be ideal for the online positioning of brands. However, in the era of social media, where worldwide penetration is increasing all the time, creating and sustaining brand trust through social communities has become a particularly difficult challenge for organizations.

According to Hootsuite's report 'The Global State of Digital in 2019', there were around 3.4 billion social media users across the globe, up from 2.7 billion in 2017, so how are organizations to reach and engage such high numbers of potential customers? North America ranks first among regions where social media is highly popular, with a social media penetration rate of 70 per cent; the second being Northern Europe at 67 per cent. Depending on when you are actually reading this book will put the figures into context, but, for the foreseeable future, the stampede of social media continues to gain speed.

Social media platforms have played a significant role in a brand's content marketing strategy by sharing information and opinions about products and services. Consumers are motivated to engage in these communities to fulfil their emotional, social, functional and relational needs. For SMBCs to be successful, there is a need for them to be based on openness, co-operation and the co-creation of value, which crucially develops trust between users.

Due to the advances in the communicative and interactive capabilities of social media, brands are able to develop their own communities which help them increase trust by enhancing brand awareness, generating positive electronic word of mouth (e-WOM), increasing consumer loyalty and achieving competitive advantages when promoting their products and services. Many of the world's biggest brands have developed brand communities through social platforms to promote and communicate their offerings to their customers and target audience. But to increase the return on the investments made in developing social communities, brands need to further understand consumers' motivations to engage and ultimately develop and sustain trust, resulting in financial and attitudinal benefits to the brand.

So why is trust so important to brands?

While being an important issue in online shopping environments, trust is arguably even more important in social media brand communities (SMBCs), where uncertainty can be higher due to the lack of face-to-face interaction and a higher level of user-generated content.

In recent times, trust has been a real issue in online environments, particularly in the wake of events such as the Cambridge Analytica data scandal of early 2018, which allegedly helped sway the outcomes of both the US election and the UK's Brexit Referendum in 2016. These controversies rightly caused public uproar, as social media users felt that they had been manipulated and deceived. It would also be an understatement to suggest recent algorithmic changes to social feeds to 'unclutter' them from unwanted content have caused issues for brands, forcing them to radically alter their marketing and engagement strategies if they want to stay relevant. Fundamentally, though, the outrage was rooted in the fact that the general public and consumers alike demand transparency from anyone they engage with – something that is crucial in determining and impacting their levels of trust.

When brands first became active on social media, product placements were so obvious that most consumers didn't pay much attention, such as Facebook's first display partnership with JP Morgan to promote Chase credit cards in 2006, for instance. However, brands soon realized that an effective method with which to strike a note with their target audience was to assimilate their product into an influencer's channels, endorsing the product at every opportunity and literally 'deciding' their followers' preferences for them. Previously, brands such as Vogue and Nike had adopted this approach utilizing the social influence of high-profile celebrities Kylie Jenner and Cristiano Ronaldo respectively, with great success.

Unfortunately for brands using this approach, consumers soon began to see through this tactic and demanded even further transparency. Indeed, Collective Bias (an influencer marketing company) recently argued only 3 per cent of consumers now care about high-profile influencer and celebrity endorsements. There's no doubt that there are challenges when it comes to developing and maintaining brand trust, with consumers becoming increasingly savvy to new approaches. However, there is light at the end of the tunnel, as this book hopes to demonstrate.

Consumers possess almost unlimited opportunities to engage with brands through social media; as such, brand social media community practices have gradually attracted more attention from businesses. Although branded websites are still the most popular places for online brand transactions and interactions, engagement through social platforms is considered a key focal point for an organization's marketing activity. However, this trend may well change, with research predicting that brand interactions on social media will soon replace traditional branded sites, so customer-oriented interactions have the potential to become much more complicated and unpredictable.

Structure of the book

Using real-life business examples and academic insight, this book reviews consumer motivation to engage with social media brand communities and the resulting opportunities for digital trust to be developed and sustained. The theoretical frameworks and psychological theories reviewed will show how effective engagement, developed via social media, can influence brand trust. This book highlights the crucial strategic considerations that brands face when engaging with their customers using social media, which vitally help develop initial and continuous digital brand trust.

The theories put forward are intended to help your organization increase its understanding of brand trust and improve any marketing and content strategies by aligning business strategy with social media platform strategy, improving consumer trust and engagement.

Understanding the potential 'value' that social media has for your brand is a unique challenge and one way of measuring return on investment is to examine what kind of corporate objectives the social media activities would satisfy. A consistent challenge for marketers has been to see how their efforts can pay off and how their social media activities can influence important brand-related variables, such as 'brand awareness'.

To further understand the influence of user-generated content in their own brand communities, an organization should make greater efforts to monitor and review any feedback received through their social communities, which will be highlighted when I discuss research strategies for brands, analysing their audience preferences through their communities. Chapters 5 and 6 also cover future considerations for brands, such as how Bitcoin and Blockchain technology can be utilized through social media activity to enhance your brand's offering.

For organizations to gain new customers and retain existing ones trust is vital. The book focuses on four key areas of interest: trust, engagement, reputation and social media. It goes on to explore the initial trust that consumers develop when they engage with a brand's social media communities for the first time, as well as the 'continual trust' that can develop through repeated social media interactions. This book aims to highlight the theoretical and managerial understanding of social media brand community engagement for brands, and how the effects of such engagement can influence consumer trust and reputation. Each chapter provides detailed insights for your business or organization and identifies which elements of a brand community can be detrimental and which can be beneficial in building a trustworthy and successful brand.

1

Branding and Digital Branding

Before we delve into consumer brand trust, it's important to first fully understand the brand concept and how it can then be applied on social media to engage effectively with customers. If we think about actual definitions, a brand can be defined as a name, term, sign, symbol, design or a combination of them, which is intended to identify the products or services of a business (or a collection of businesses) to differentiate them from rival organizations. But most of all, a brand is, or at least should be, the positive image that you want your organization to have. In terms of understanding what a brand means to customers, Amazon founder Jeff Bezos summed it up brilliantly when he said: 'A brand for a company is like a reputation for a person; you earn reputation by trying to do hard things well.'

As an organization or individual, you can control your brand but essentially it doesn't belong to you. It belongs to the customer who experiences your company, which is why organizations have to work so hard to continuously ensure any brand experience is a positive one. In order to achieve this, successful organizations never rest on their brand laurels. As former Starbucks Chief Marketing Officer Scott Bedbury said: 'A great brand is a story that is never completely told.'

This is such an exciting quote for any organization to apply to their brand. Your brand changes as your business does and also with the new technologies you use to promote your brand story to keep it interesting for customers. But there is also an emotional side to branding. From a consumer perspective, your brand is the conveyor of an emotive brand story and should act as a foundation for developing close customer relationships.

In contrast, the cultural side of branding takes into account the sociocultural perspective of the brand construct. A theory used in psychology, the sociocultural perspective describes the awareness of circumstances affecting individuals and how their behaviours are influenced by social and cultural factors. The sociocultural perspective considers the different ways in which individuals engage and interact with their peers and social groups and how these groups can affect their thoughts and feelings. This perspective is really interesting for businesses ready to put their brand out there on social media as it applies to so much of our daily routine: how we communicate and understand one another, as well as our mental and emotional states of mind. This theory links really well to another famous brand quote from Bezos: 'Your brand is what people say about you when you are not in the room.' Essentially, this means your organization should always try to ensure that it behaves or acts in a way which encourages people to say positive things about you when you're not there to hear it.

The significant changes introduced by the Internet have impacted strategic brand processes for organizations. In the past, consumers have had little influence on organizational strategy with information being provided to them using traditional methods. Then, brands had complete control over what consumers 'thought' they knew about them. Due to the limited access to available information and in some instances geographical constraints, engagement with customers was at best minimal and organizations were able to influence customers how they saw fit. However, with the Internet being utilized for commercial purposes, this approach is no longer viable or beneficial to organizations. Historically, a firm's brand activity was focused on the corporate offering which allowed a 'one-way' form of communication, such as a campaign billboard. The main downside to this approach is that there's no opportunity for the consumer to give feedback to the brand. However, the Internet and subsequent social platforms created further opportunities for 'two-way' (brand-consumer) and even 'three-way' (brand-consumer-customer) communication, which has led companies to re-evaluate their brand strategic model.

The value of knowing the difference between a customer and a consumer is crucial when determining the marketing strategy for your product or service. Often the terms are used interchangeably but in basic terms a customer is the individual/entity who buys the product or service. For example, a supermarket chain buying products for re-sale is a customer, whereas a consumer is the individual/entity who actually uses your product or service – i.e., the individual who consumes products from a supermarket. Of course, a customer can also be a consumer if they purchase the product or service and then consume it.

For instance, aggregation websites such as TripAdvisor provide consumers with extensive product/service details as well as brand consumer experiences, making customers considerably more informed when making their purchase decisions. A perfect example of this is Skyscanner, the travel fare aggregator website and travel metasearch engine, which has over 70 million monthly active users operating in over 65 markets. Skyscanner's success is built on using data and measurement analysis to help their customers achieve their travelling goals. In order for Skyscanner to grow, the company's mind-set is focused on an experimentation culture by engaging with customers. Their approach of 'design like you're right, test like you're wrong' is based on customer insight through user research and then predicting what product changes will have the most effective impact. Rik Higham, Senior Product Manager for Skyscanner, explains: 'Our culture of hypothesis-driven experimentation is so important and so successful because it allows anyone at Skyscanner to quickly test an idea. We no longer spend months creating a feature that may or may not work. Instead we test lots of small ideas, all based on insights and data, to see what potential they have. The more ideas we test, the more we learn about travellers, and the more informed our future tests are.' Essentially this is a 'peer review' process which Skyscanner has in place to ensure visibility for customers; there is continuous two-way knowledge sharing between the organization and their target audience. This peer review process is one of Skyscanner's brand values, which can help shape the direction of any organization.

Brand values

No matter the size of your organization, the values you choose to embody your business will have an impact on communications and most importantly, your relationships and connections with your target audience. Your brand values will influence consumer buying decisions and affect your sales and profits as consumers are more likely to buy from a brand whose values are similar to their own. Successful brands choose their values carefully and integrate them into every aspect of their organization to keep moving forward. By investing the time to establish and communicate your brand values, you are making a commitment concerning what is important to your organization and what you feel is important to your customers.

So where to start when defining or re-evaluating your core values? Well, your values must be true to what you believe in, who you are and what is important to you and your brand. Don't worry if your organization has long established values as defining brand values is not a one-off task but a process that needs regular review to ensure values remain consistent to what your organization represents. Often, brands project values based on what others feel they should be, which won't be sustainable in the long run. As an exercise, write down your own brand definition and include the values that your organization has or aspires to have. To help get you started, one of Google's core values is highlighted below:

It's best to do one thing really, really well.

> 'We do search. With one of the world's largest research groups focused exclusively on solving search problems, we know what we do well, and how we could do it better. Through continued iteration on difficult problems, we've been able to solve complex issues and provide continuous improvements to a service that already makes finding information a fast and seamless experience for millions of people. Our dedication to improving search helps us apply what we've learned to new products, like Gmail and Google Maps. Our hope is to bring the power of search to previously unexplored areas, and to help people access and use even more of the ever-expanding information in their lives.' (Google.com, 2019)

Once you have a clear understanding of what your brand represents, you can start to consider additional brand management perspectives, such as the emotional and cultural approach to your branding and the values your brand possesses or aspires to represent. Once you've done that, below are some more exercises you can work on individually or as a team to establish or refine your brand values.

And the award goes to … How do you want to be remembered?

Imagine you're receiving a lifetime achievement award at an awards ceremony and what the introductory speech before you arrive on stage might be. What would you want the guest speaker to say about your character and what your work and achievements have represented? You can then look for regular themes which can help establish your main brand values. Continuing with the lifetime award speech theme, write down the names of brands you want your organization to be like and who you'd like to work alongside, or be mentioned with in the speech. For each organization, think of one aspect of their brand that represents them and use those aspects to develop your values. Finally, for the award speech, imagine the part where they cut away to a video feed of someone who has worked with you and what they'd say. For established companies you can send out questionnaires to customers and ask them to highlight the values that best represent you and your brand and research the existing feelings that they have for your brand.

Now that you have a selection of your core values, you can define what they mean and represent to you and to your brand. There's no denying this will be a challenging task, as it requires complete transparency and honesty with yourself and your team to determine what is important to the organization. However, once you have clarity on your values, your decision-making will hugely improve as for every strategic decision you make, you will be able to refer back to your core values for guidance. This is particularly true in terms of collaborative opportunities, hiring the right staff and building customer relationships. If your activity does not reflect your values, you could face the risk of feeling anxious and frustrated. Your employees and customers would also recognize the lack of consistency and unfulfilled promises, which in turn could negatively impact your brand reputation.

Once you have established your brand values, your entire organization must operate in alignment with those values, demonstrating them in day-to-day activity and crucially, in all communications with customers. Adopting this approach and applying the values to your business will motivate employees to share your beliefs and customers who share your values will be attracted to the idea of engaging with your brand. When you trust what your organization stands for and trust your team to promote those brand values, only then can you begin to engage with customers through social communities and truly highlight what your brand stands for within any digital environment.

Digital branding

Having covered the traditional branding concepts, we're now going to review the strategic understanding of digital branding. Before delving a little deeper into the possibilities and considerations, let's look at a definition. Digital branding can be viewed as an organization's identity, values and credibility presented through digital platforms.

Digital branding is a brand management technique that combines branding and digital marketing over a range of digital platforms, which cover Internet-based relationships, device-based applications or media content. Essentially, digital branding aims to utilize an organization's digital assets to connect and create lasting relationships. The main digital assets that you need to develop, promote and manage to create a strong trustworthy brand are:

- websites (including blogs and online stores);
- social media channels and assets;
- multi-media content assets;
- mobile assets, including apps and mobile sites;
- digital databases, including email subscribers.

Digital branding is a term used to cover the variety of ways in which a business stands out to customers online. This can include a number of different marketing functions, such as social media, content marketing, SEO (search engine optimization) and online advertising, as well as influencer marketing. So essentially digital branding is about developing and establishing your brand's story and offering online.

You may often hear the terms 'digital marketing' and 'digital branding' used alongside one another but in practice they are quite different. Digital marketing is concerned with promoting a particular service or product by highlighting its features or benefits, whereas digital branding aims to highlight the underlying beliefs and core values of the organization.

Once you have developed your digital assets, the next hurdle – and one of the most important – is ensuring your digital brand is easily visible so that new leads and customers can find your company, review your content and then finally decide to trust your organization enough to purchase your products or services. Effective marketing can no longer rely on just one channel, as your target audience will, in all likelihood, use a variety of different social channels. Successful digital branding requires multi-channel digital marketing strategies and tactics, which include:

- search engine optimization (SEO);
- paid digital advertising (this includes banner ads and Google Ads);

- social media marketing;
- email marketing.

Digital marketing can be highly effective for one-time buyers using a limited promotion, for example, but having a strong digital brand will help develop relationships between your company and your customers. When looking to define your digital brand and marketing strategies, you must be acutely aware of the objectives for each one. For instance, when carrying out marketing activity using digital platforms, you are at the same time researching your audience and competitors, creating product/service interest, generating demand and promoting your offering. Whereas when working on brand strategy, you are raising brand awareness, providing quality service to your target audience and creating brand equity, which describes your brand's value. That value is determined by consumer perception of, and experiences with, your brand – so if people think highly of your brand, it has a positive brand equity.

Devising an effective brand strategy is all about showcasing the value of your offering and your brand identity. Your brand identity allows consumers to instantly recognize your brand through the visible elements of a brand (such as colours, design, logotype, name and symbol), which together identify and distinguish your brand in the mind of the consumer. McDonald's brand identity, for instance, is instantly recognizable and its uniformity and consistent offering has contributed to its success.

It's important to remember that digital marketing is more focused on promoting an organization's product or service based on its quality, and an innovative and creative digital marketing campaign carried out well has the potential to inspire, inform, entertain and attract new audiences to a brand. However, a firm's brand will ordinarily still be visible to consumers long after a product or service has been removed or replaced. It is the initial impression and lasting memory that is important to consumers, so while both can be utilized to attract one-time buyers, branding is more effective in creating long-lasting relationships between businesses and customers.

Don't forget your logo!

Obviously, your brand is so much more than a logo, but there is no getting away from the fact that it is a huge part of your organization, which can often be overlooked in terms of developing trust. Your logo encapsulates your identity and while the most effective logos are simple and consistent, they must be robust enough to fit different sizes, moods, events or even occasions. When creating or re-evaluating your brand identity, consider how your brand identity will be presented. Think how the font you choose will be viewed on a small screen, have accessible web brand colours, and think about website and mobile load times as well as content readability for search engines.

To stand out from competitors your brand logo and identity must leap off tablet or smartphone screens as well as from Web and social media sites. Your brand needs to go digital first to ensure consistency, so the logo will have to work on multiple screens. For instance, be mindful of accessibility issues (e.g. navigation or site structure) for your audience, as well as using Web-safe fonts (fonts that are likely to be present on the majority of computer systems) and imagery that works well online, as well as logos that work on mobile phones. By adopting a digital-first approach you can optimize your customer's digital experience but also remain true to your brand values, ensuring your chosen brand colours, fonts and imagery work effectively on digital platforms. However, colours and iconography may also impact page load times, which is something else to bear in mind.

Rather than developing different digital versions of your brand for your website, think about how your brand will look on social media sites as well and consider how it can evolve to provide an outstanding digital experience. One great example of collective brand logo planning is the digital media service provider Netflix, who have mastered the art of branding. Netflix created a brand logo that brings the brand together at every digital touchpoint in any format and in any size. So, look at your current brand logo: would it work just as well on a huge billboard in New York's Times Square as it does as a Facebook profile image? If so, you are on the right track and if it doesn't, there is definitely potential to review your design. But even if for the moment you are quite happy with your brand logo, look at how some organizations use logo design as another method to engage with customers. Google's constant iterations of their logo and Airbnb's invitation to consumers to customize their logo provides customers with the opportunity to really engage with brands and open up avenues of trust. Airbnb's brand logo has previously been made available for anyone to modify and create their own version, which shows that the brand trusts that their customers know and understand their values, which are represented in their designs.

Brand visibility

Whether you are a personal or business brand, the challenge today is to become and remain visible in a digital world filled with constant noise, endless information and increasing competition. While a stand-out logo will help, to reach as many potential customers as possible while still engaging with existing ones, a multi-channel digital brand identity is necessary. Spread across suitable channels – and it's important to recognize not every channel will be appropriate for your brand – your brand message needs to be consistent and requires diligent management and dedicated resource to be a success. Nobody said this was going to be easy, but if you are willing to put in the hard hours, it can be incredibly rewarding for your business.

Everyone is well aware of the importance of search engine ranking. If you are not discoverable on a search engine then this really difficult task of becoming a trustworthy brand just became a lot harder. The goal for every brand is to be the number one ranking on Google when a customer begins a search, which is a key trust indicator, given Google's reputation and position. This can be achieved with an excellent website with strong search engine optimization (SEO) content and an effective Google Ads strategy. Google Ads (formerly known as Google AdWords) is Google's own advertising service that allows organizations to place search results for their website on a search engine results page (SERP) by paying for them. However, this book will focus on how your digital brand strategy can utilize social media channels for engagement and trust development.

Brand communities

As consumers become aware of brand communities and use them as part of their daily lives, organizations need to evolve their focus from product branding to corporate branding to be part of that daily routine. The rise of social media opened up a new avenue for brands to connect with consumers more directly and more organically. Due to this rise, customers have started to develop an interest in brands and are eager to find out more about the ideals and values of that organization. What better way to do this than to join a brand community?

A brand community is created from a variety of relationships that members develop with a brand, product, marketers and other consumers. Brand communities can perform many important functions on behalf of the brand, such as providing assistance or informing customers of new product developments. Consequently, brand communities are an increasingly vital part of brand management strategies and consistently look to integrate themselves with consumer daily routines.

Though social media platforms are considered particularly suitable for developing customer relationships, it is the increased role of social media that has created a need for customer engagement. Brand communities provide an important platform for customer engagement behaviours (which will be discussed in more detail in Chapter 3), which in turn can be utilized by firms to engage with their customers and further brand visibility. Community participation from a brand is focused on engaging with loyal customers, influencing members' perceptions about the brand, disseminating information and learning from and about customers. This form of customer engagement is directly related to the emergence of new media and all the new ways in which customers can interact with firms, covering both purchase and non-purchase behaviour. Such an engagement is considered a behavioural manifestation towards the brand or firm that goes beyond transactions, which also includes all consumer-to-firm interactions and consumer-to-consumer communications about the brand. We will cover engagement in more detail in Chapter 2, so for now let's focus on how brand communities are formed.

Brand community features

A study by Muniz and O'Guinn in 2001 highlighted that social communities have three core commonalities: consciousness of kind, rituals and traditions and moral responsibility.

- **consciousness of kind** is the intrinsic connection that members feel towards one another and the collective sense of difference from others not in the community;

- **shared rituals and traditions** represent the vital social processes by which the meaning of the community is reproduced and transmitted within and beyond the community. For instance, sharing brand experiences and building upon the history of the brand, which develops the culture of the community;
- **sense of moral responsibility** refers to the sense of duty or obligation to the community as a whole and to its individual members.

Brand communities can often be classified as organic or inorganic; where organic communities are created and hosted by consumers to discuss experiences, inorganic communities are created and influenced by the brands themselves. Regardless, communities allow consumers the opportunity to share both positive and negative experiences whenever they have interacted or engaged with the brand. So, in some instances brand-initiated communities may not display negative opinions regarding service, experience or product performances and companies may choose to remove or block this kind of content from the community. We'll discuss how this is a terrible strategic move later in the book. Before delving into strategic digital branding or trust considerations for organizations, it's important to acknowledge the ways in which social media has impacted community growth and development.

Social Media Brand Communities

Most people we know are actively involved in social media brand communities (SMBC). A study put forward by Habibi, Laroche and Richard (2014) argued that there are five dimensions that make a social media brand community (SMBC) unique compared to other communities and these are outlined in Figure 1.

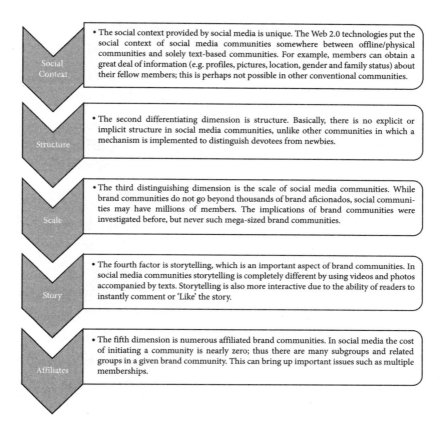

- The social context provided by social media is unique. The Web 2.0 technologies put the social context of social media communities somewhere between offline/physical communities and solely text-based communities. For example, members can obtain a great deal of information (e.g. profiles, pictures, location, gender and family status) about their fellow members; this is perhaps not possible in other conventional communities.

- The second differentiating dimension is structure. Basically, there is no explicit or implicit structure in social media communities, unlike other communities in which a mechanism is implemented to distinguish devotees from newbies.

- The third distinguishing dimension is the scale of social media communities. While brand communities do not go beyond thousands of brand aficionados, social communities may have millions of members. The implications of brand communities were investigated before, but never such mega-sized brand communities.

- The fourth factor is storytelling, which is an important aspect of brand communities. In social media communities storytelling is completely different by using videos and photos accompanied by texts. Storytelling is also more interactive due to the ability of readers to instantly comment or 'Like' the story.

- The fifth dimension is numerous affiliated brand communities. In social media the cost of initiating a community is nearly zero; thus there are many subgroups and related groups in a given brand community. This can bring up important issues such as multiple memberships.

FIGURE 1 *The five dimensions that make a social media brand community unique*

Organic reach on social media is how well your posts perform without any advertising spend behind them. With the consistent algorithm changes at Facebook, Instagram and Twitter, organic reach is increasingly losing ground within social media environments, so brands that are proactive and create communities with engaged fans enjoy the advantages of customer recommendations. However, each brand is unique, and while Figure 1 provides a framework for a brand's social media strategy, what worked for one organization can be very difficult to reproduce for another. At the core of any successful SMBC strategy is an absolute commitment to your personality so that you can create a truly authentic customer experience. This experience forms a key part of your digital branding strategy.

Digital branding strategy

Apple, Coca-Cola and Adidas are some of the best-known global brands around, all of which have been operating successfully for a number of years. A history of effective business decisions, popular products, as well as significant investment have gone into building and maintaining these brands. But crucially in the digital branding landscape, they applied their brand strategy across all of their platforms. Creating or developing a brand identity and a plan to reach your audience has never been more important than it is today. Unfortunately, the reason why so many organizations' digital branding strategies fail is due to a lack of cohesion between all of their digital activities. Smaller organizations sometimes fall victim to this approach due to resource constraints or they outsource key elements of their digital operations. For instance, they may have a separate organization hosting their website, with an agency running their social media communities, but digital advertising may be carried out in-house. With so much disconnected activity, it can be extremely difficult to maintain a centralized digital brand and marketing strategy, which is why digital brand management is so crucial and effective digital branding campaigns are vital for any successful business.

Your digital branding strategy will guide activity that will increase your brand's presence, but it will also enable you to develop trust through much stronger relationships with your customers and target audience. The ability to promote your brand across a number of different channels has many advantages for your business, but essentially, it increases the reach of your messages and allows them to meaningfully engage with your target audience. But there are a number of factors you must plan for before adopting such an approach.

First, multi-channel marketing requires the right tools and platforms to analyse success and failure of campaigns. You will also need to know what is being said about your brand to mitigate potential PR issues. To prepare for these scenarios you can manage and monitor your mentions through social media analytics platforms, which can be managed in-house or through other agencies.

Two further considerations when formulating strategy must include the design and positioning of your brand. The design elements include the creative materials that distinguish your organization's digital channels, such as the social media banners and digital advertising images; the 'positioning' concerns the actual communication being delivered through your digital channels. Aside from things like design and imagery, positioning also covers the tone of the messaging: for example, whether your tweets are informal and humorous or encourage comment, or they are more formal and one-way in a bid to share reliable news and information.

The next stage is to identify ways in which to apply your brand's offering using the different benefits that digital channels can provide. Digital brand positioning is all about using digital channels to differentiate your brand from any competitors and thus leave a positive lasting impression with customers. When developing your digital brand positioning strategy, the main aim is to create brand associations in consumers' minds so that they perceive your brand as being positive and different. Some of the main digital considerations that you can adopt when formulating your multichannel strategy can include:

- **Search ranking**: Rankings in search engine optimization (SEO) refers to a website's position in the search engine results page. There are a number of ranking factors that influence whether a website appears higher on the search engine results page (SERP) attributed to the content relevance to the search term, or the quality of backlinks pointing to the page. Ranking factors play a massive role in SEO and the overall digital marketing strategy for a brand. SEO, in particular, is a specific discipline focused on the optimizations needed to have a technically sound website domain and providing content that is relevant to users and ultimately attracts the right target audience to your business.

- **Paid digital advertising**: From pay-per-click (PPC) ads with Google to image ads with Facebook, there are numerous opportunities to promote your brand to targeted audiences. Paid advertising is another key component of digital branding and one of the only ways to guarantee that you get in front of your chosen audience. While it can be expensive for organizations, it is one of the fastest ways to promote your brand to consumers with whom you want to engage.

- **Mobile/tablet optimization**: Nearly everyone has access to a smartphone or tablet nowadays and so ensuring your content is responsive (i.e. it adapts easily to the screen size and resolution) is a necessity. Consumers will go back to their search results very quickly if your content is not optimized for mobile platforms, which in turn has an immediate and negative impact on your brand perception.

- **Chatbots**: Due to advances in artificial intelligence (AI), chatbots are now digital customer service tools for brands that can provide instantaneous responses to customer queries.

- **Video**: No longer the up-and-coming digital marketing tactic everyone was talking about a few years ago, video is very much here to stay. Its dominance across digital channels is undeniable and growth continues apace. Consumers want to see more video content from brands and such content is capable of providing a strong return on investment (ROI).

- **Viral**: Going viral isn't necessarily something that can be planned or created, it may occur as a result of planned marketing effort, but is not something that can be specified when formulating marketing objectives. Put simply, all you have to do is something that's never been done before, which sounds like a pretty daunting statement, but never one that should be dismissed when planning a campaign.

Effective digital brand positioning requires a thorough understanding and awareness of your target audience, your brand and your competitors' positioning so that you can create a distinct brand image that resonates with consumers. This seems straightforward enough but in reality, it's not that easy. Consumers are bombarded with messages every day, which makes it even more important to ensure your brand positioning is on the money.

As with traditional marketing, organizations need a strong value proposition across all digital channels to ensure their messages stand out. Mindful of this necessity, your organization must consistently review three areas to assist in brand positioning.

1. Adaptability

Digital environments and community platforms are constantly changing so it's crucial that organizations are aware of new technologies, which can strengthen their digital brand management, with a willingness to invest time and resources in such technology.

2. Personalization

The most successful brands interact with customers in a personalized, one-to-one basis using their digital platforms. One obvious example of successful personalization is Amazon. Its personalization strategy isn't exactly new and, since 2013, its product curation and recommendation algorithm have been used to great effect. The key benefit for Amazon is that this often leads to unplanned purchases, which in turn has led to numerous businesses imitating Amazon's online shopping experience for customers.

3. Analytics

Social community analytics provide valuable insights about your target audience and how they engage with your brand digitally, allowing you to create and refine your digital brand presence and increase community members. Digital branding success involves integrating online activity with offline brand events. Behind the ad campaigns and creative promotional materials, the basic intention of any offline marketing strategy is usually to increase online traffic, overall sales and profits. There are various strategies companies can employ to achieve these results, such as direct mail campaigns, loyalty schemes or discount pricing. However, an integrated approach is key as opposed to just seeing digital as a quick way of delivering content or a means to measure impact. The overall aim should be to provide a unique and consistent brand experience aligned with your brand's strategy, positioning and purpose.

While so much emphasis is on social media, your organization's website also underpins your digital branding strategy. Everyone is already well aware of this, I'm sure, as no matter what industry you are in, a fully functioning website is vital for online commerce. Websites play a huge role in digital branding as they are often the main 'shop window' to help new and existing customers learn more about your business. For this factor alone, it is crucial that your organization's website reflects your brand values. While functionality is paramount to showcase products, process sales and generate leads, the website must always indicate what your brand stands for. One great example of this is the Dropbox website. Dropbox uses simple, straightforward language to explain its functions and seizes every opportunity to reassure visitors with statistics and graphics to build credibility and develop trust with consumers.

Remarkable content focus

Having a content strategy is also a key component for any digital branding strategy. For many businesses the issue is that their content is either focused purely on product/service promotion, or they create random content which doesn't align with the brand values or business objectives. The content focus must always link to your organization's digital marketing objectives, but we'll look at this in more detail when we review engagement strategies in Chapter 3.

Having a clear understanding of the existing technologies, and their capabilities, gives marketing teams the freedom to design engaging content experiences and crucially develop relationships. This is what market-leading brands do: they seek to excite and inform with all of their content to make their brand 'remarkable'. A brand's content can't just stand out and be interesting, though: it needs to inspire visitors to get involved by liking, sharing or making a 'remark' to truly engage with them.

Effective digital brands start with stories and continue to tell them to keep customers interested in them. It's fair to say that consumers aren't excited about general business operations and activity – for instance, how many of your favourite brands' annual reports have you ever read? But consumers do get excited about the story behind the business activity and learning how your organization sees things differently. It's vital that the content you produce tells your brand story but also resonates with consumers on some level, whether emotionally or intellectually, and providing content that hits these marks helps create loyalty among customers who share the brand's values.

It is crucial for your brand to have one overarching brand management strategy that applies to all channels of marketing for both offline and digital. In other words, the brand values that you wish to communicate must be consistent no matter what method you use to promote them. Nevertheless, having a successful digital brand strategy requires effective management and a continual review of your strategic approach and activity.

Digital brand management

Now let's look at digital brand management, how to do it well and why it's so important for organizations. Digital brand management is a combination of policies which directly or indirectly influence the way your target audience interacts with your brand online. This can include your approach to landing page content, (i.e. content for a web page, which has been created specifically for a marketing or advertising campaign) apps, social media, blog marketing, PPC (pay-per-click advertising) and anything that is promoted using a digital platform.

Like traditional marketing practices, successful digital brand management depends on consistency. Successful global brands such as Nike, Amazon and Apple have applied relentless consistency across all channels so that their products/services are instantly recognizable to consumers who are aware of their brand values. Not all companies will have the budgets of these huge brands when handling their brand management. However, using their approach as a benchmark as well as establishing clear brand guidelines with a clear brand identity in digital environments can help position your brand successfully.

We live in a highly digitized time, and especially for millennials it feels as though we've been connected and communicating online forever, with organizations' digital landscapes constantly evolving as new platforms and devices appear on the market. As the ways we connect and communicate evolve, so too do the ways in which businesses share their brand message and values and create new customer experiences. To stay competitive, your organization can't stand still; constant review of digital brand management is essential.

One great example of flexible and adaptive digital brand management was that of Budweiser's 2016 World Series campaign. Working with an external social media agency, VaynerMedia, Budweiser's sports marketing teams developed a strategy to capitalize on the possibility that the Chicago Cubs could win the World Series, something for which their fans had been waiting an awfully long time. The Budweiser team knew that this could be a moving and powerful occasion, one not just Cubs fans but sports fans across the globe would remember. There was always the possibility that the Cubs could of course lose, but the idea that they would be so close to making dreams reality provided an incredible opportunity to create something unique and memorable. The Budweiser team weren't naive enough to think they would be the only brand planning something around this event, so they needed to create and manage a digital strategy that would stand out through authenticity and effective all-important timing. To jump out from their competitors would require incredible storytelling, utilizing the real-time benefits of YouTube. What was the end result? Well, their advert had over 3 million views, but how did they do it?

They applied three different digital brand management perspectives to their campaign, incorporating: *the Brand Approach* – being part of the fans' experience and celebrating authenticity; *the Creative Approach* – effective planning with an instant impact, and finally, *the Media Approach* – launching the campaign with a digital-first methodology and optimizing as the campaign went on.

The Brand Approach

When reviewing the brand perspective, Budweiser wanted to remind fans of the brand's long-standing relationship with the Chicago Cubs and baseball in general. However, at the same time, the organization didn't want fans to feel as if they were being sold to during a memorable moment. For Budweiser it wasn't just about selling more of their products, rather giving fans a story with which to remember something special. Working with VaynerMedia, YouTube and MLB, Budweiser researched and analysed its own history with the game to find the answer.

The Creative Approach

The next step was to review the creative side, plan and establish a hook for fans. Budweiser's creative strategy was to deliver a viral-ready fan reaction video the moment the game ended. Nevertheless, as we've already mentioned, the greatest challenge was preparing for each eventuality. They didn't know who would win so would have to prepare for both a Cubs and an Indians win scenario, which meant creating two different videos.

Once the result was determined, VaynerMedia had to rush to edit the Cubs' fans reactions, link to their social accounts and run TrueView ads to promote it on YouTube. The first few seconds of the video were vital to capture fans' emotion so the video started with an inspiring 1991 clip of well-known sportscaster Harry Caray predicting the Cubs' future. 'As sure as God made green apples,' he says, looking into the camera, 'one day the Chicago Cubs are gonna be in the World Series.' Predicting the future and it becoming reality made for an incredible hook.

The Media Approach

Finally, from a media perspective, the approach was to focus the launch using a digital-first approach and optimize along the way. This wasn't an approach that Budweiser had used historically, but from the start of the campaign through effective research, they knew YouTube would be the right platform to launch the campaign. YouTube gave Budweiser the potential to create a video full of immersive, emotional and engaging content that was a perfect fit for the celebration. Budweiser hit the right balance of paid and earned media with this campaign by front-loading their media spend in the first 48 hours the ad was live, then letting organic buzz develop from there. The organization then used real-time analytics to analyse which version was resonating with the most fans. By then pinpointing the best-performing ad, they could focus their advertising spend on supporting the most compelling video for maximum exposure. The results were hugely positive and the campaign was a massive success for the brand.

Now, your brand may not have the same budget or resources that are available to Budweiser, but the approach used by them for this campaign can be applied to how you manage your digital brand as well. The campaign was successful because they knew what their audience was passionate about, discussed ideas and challenges and conducted consumer research. Finally, they planned their timelines and determined the best platform to help achieve their objectives. But crucially, they were authentic with their message and it was both different and memorable. When formulating your next campaign, remember authenticity is key to being remembered.

Ever since the social network phenomenon began in the early 2000s, brands have attempted to create intriguing and memorable adverts that consumers would be motivated to share online. Advertising agencies are often asked about the possibility of content going viral, followed by sighs from agents due to the difficulty of actually achieving this. Going 'viral' can be fantastic for organizations, as it allows maximum exposure in a short period of time. While it can be misused or go horribly wrong – e.g. Pepsi's Kendall Jenner political protest ad of 2017 that received widespread criticism – it can also be of huge benefit to businesses even though, recently, there has been a considerable decline in the popularity of this method to promote brands online, mostly due to the annoyance of 'clickbait', (content that is designed to attract attention and encourage visitors to click on a link to a web page). It is still one of the most high-risk/high-reward activities that your brand can attempt.

It shouldn't come as a huge surprise to hear that the NFL Super Bowl has a lot to do with ads becoming viral. As one of the biggest, and most watched, sporting events in the world, it has become synonymous with huge creative campaigns from global brands. Amazon and Netflix recently utilized this platform to launch their own campaigns. The Amazon Echo allows you to verbally interact with a virtual assistant called Alexa to carry out a number of different actions, such as answer questions, play music or plan your daily schedule. During the Super Bowl of 2018, Amazon launched the 'Alexa has lost her voice' campaign. The ad presented the idea that Alexa had lost her voice, which was then was replaced by celebrity voices such as Michelin-starred Gordon Ramsay answering culinary questions. Whether intentional or not, this video encouraged a wide range of parodies, becoming a viral Internet meme sensation. Similarly, Netflix capitalized on the Super Bowl's popularity with their Cloverfield Paradox Marketing Campaign. Here, Netflix didn't just make a post or a video in the hope that it went viral, but instead they made a movie that is available on the platform go viral. So how did they do something that's never been done before? Instead of putting out adverts for the movie release date, they immediately released it on their platform. There was no need for viewers to wait; instead of building anticipation like other trailers, they capitalized on the instant interest that the advert generated.

The reason this viral marketing campaign was a success was because it incorporated a number of factors. They demonstrated confidence in their product in that they are not reliant on Hollywood studios. Netflix also utilized social media, by releasing the trailer on all of their platforms, which meant that excitement would generate among followers and reviewers would have to drop what they were doing to watch the film and post their review as soon as possible in order to maintain their own brand.

Whether a viral Super Bowl commercial or influencer marketing campaign involving A-list celebrities, your brand can take note from these great campaigns and consider how you can get creative with your brand – which is why social media is such a good leveller for all brands, regardless of size.

Branding summary

A successful digital brand needs a consistent, well-thought-out strategy and effective management, which includes a wide range of online activities integrated with offline brand activity. An integrated approach is key to providing great content and an easy way of measuring effectiveness. The overall aim should be to deliver an authentic and consistent total brand experience aligned with your brand's strategy, positioning and purpose.

With platforms such as Instagram, Twitter and Facebook you don't need a bottomless marketing budget to create and run a successful marketing campaign. You just have to understand who your audience are, put yourself in their shoes and anticipate what they would think is funny, cool or interesting. We'll look into this in more detail in Chapter 3, but it's just as important to remember that it's not all about the amount you have in your budget: it comes down to ideas, planning and execution.

Brands now live, breathe and thrive in the digital age, adapting to a world that is changing faster each day. As Ray Kurzweil, Engineering Director of Google, said, 'We won't experience 100 years of progress in the 21st century – it will be more like 20,000 years of progress at today's rate in the 21st century.' Success in today's industries relies on how brands handle their identity on digital platforms. The overall customer experience and the sharing of that experience are what define a brand. Your brand is one of your organization's greatest assets and should tell your target audience exactly what to expect if they decide to use your products or services. It is symbolic of your identity and values and by being open and honest with your offering you can develop and sustain trusting relationships with customers.

Before you can develop your brand identity, you need a thorough understanding of the core values for your business, what sets you apart and how you are superior to your competitors. Your brand positioning is crucial and you must ensure that what you want to tell your target audience about your brand is consistent with their actual wants and needs and what you can deliver. A strong brand identity will attract new customers by stressing the differences between you and competitors – vital if you are in a highly competitive or fast-moving market where it is difficult to differentiate yourself on just your products' features. Your digital marketing must wholly support your brand identity across all the channels you choose to utilize, emphasizing your brand values through everything you do.

2

Trust

Now that we've reviewed the intricacies and nuances of the brand concept, we can look at how consumer trust can be applied to brands by analysing what exactly trust is and how it is formed.

Trust is the one thing that is relevant across all consumer generations for brands. It is universal and the one feature that can be applied to all cultures – 'When the trust account is high, communication is easy, instant, and effective.' This quote, from Stephen R. Covey, successful businessman and author of the bestselling book, *The 7 Habits of Highly Effective People*, encapsulates why organizations must be so focused on developing consumer trust in their brand because never before has the average consumer held so much sway. Whether your company is business-to-consumer (B2C), business-to-business (B2B), a small- to medium-sized enterprise (SME) start-up or a global brand, you will discover the same challenges that all organizations face: attracting new prospects, retaining existing customers, generating leads, improving your search ranking and improving brand loyalty. There is also the added demand for brands to be innovative, respond to consumers' queries, take responsibility for errors and in some cases provide social commentary on brand-related issues. All these aspects are crucial to succeeding in business, but they are based on one all-important foundation: consumer trust.

With social media at our fingertips, thanks to the mobile and tablet boom, consumers can share their opinions whenever they wish, making brand trust so vital to organizations. Social media business communities can have a significantly positive impact on trust for your brand. For instance, SMBCs can relay information a lot quicker than traditional channels and when accurate information is a key factor in developing and establishing trust, this gives brands a huge competitive advantage. The cost benefits for organizations are obvious due to the relative ease of exploring new audiences and markets through social media. However, with the sheer volume of social media messages that consumers are exposed to each day, it's fair to say that they are highly cynical when it comes to giving out their trust. Only certain industries provide the option for customers to actually try a product before they purchase it, so they are then faced with the task of finding alternative sources of information before they decide to make a purchase. One such source lies within social media communities and for online commerce in particular, social media has changed the ways in which consumers and brands interact, providing a platform to develop relationships and giving consumers a more influential voice when it comes to trust development.

Due to the higher number of uncertain aspects in online commerce, the creation and development of brand trust is extremely important and also extremely difficult. Often online shoppers do not have face-to-face contact with the brand representative or fellow consumers and because of the nuances of online commerce, there are increasing levels of unethical or illegal behaviour. An online vendor can take payment but deliver a poor-quality or completely different product from that displayed, or may not provide the product or service at all.

With such uncertainty connected to social media, look at the challenges facing your organization from your target audience's perspective. They typically have the ability to visit countless websites and SMBCs offering and promoting similar services or products to your own. Why should they use your business instead of your competitor's? Will they definitely receive good service or products at a fair value price? Put simply, can they trust your brand to deliver on your promise?

If consumers don't feel that they can trust your brand this may be due to the fact that you are not promoting how trustworthy you actually are. Most brands will tell customers that their business is credible and trustworthy, but again due to the sheer volume, without further validation consumers just won't believe it. So you can legitimately ask yourself, is your brand doing enough to make people trust you and is this reflected in your marketing and communications strategy? But before you ask yourself this, let's look at how trust can be defined and is created.

Consumer trust development

The big question for brands around trust is how to create and sustain it. It's important to consider how trust is actually defined and how it is formed before we look at the stages of trust development and strategies for your business to increase digital brand trust.

Trust is a psychological state of mind that is multi-dimensional and comprised of factors such as expectancy, faith, control, consistency and risk. Each of these factors describes the way trust works as a personal cognitive response, to a person, object or situation. However, trust is a lot more than a psychological state of mind and to fully understand consumer trust, brands must accept that trust for their target audience combines both a psychological and sociological perspective. Trust development evolves through cognitive processes or stages that are dependent on a social structure and time and it is the cornerstone for every business transaction and all consumer behaviour.

But as vital as it is for brands, the fundamental concept of trust is difficult to pin down as each consumer has different trust measures. As individuals, we tend to develop trust on intuition, not just in everyday interactions with people but at a place of work or when making a purchase. This works in general and helps us develop trusting relationships, but when it comes to developing brand trust there are many more opportunities to leverage trust with your target audience. Having a strong awareness of the staged process or systematic approach to the process of building and sustaining trust will have a number of business advantages for your organization.

The stages of trust

Brands that increase their understanding of the stages of trust are able to learn how it can grow, change and decline. When it comes to trust in professional or transactional relationships, there are generally three types of trust, which are linked and sequential:

- **Calculus-based trust** is focused on the fear of punishment for violating trust that we experience, but also in the rewards for preserving it. Here, trust is based on a calculation that we make in terms of comparing the costs and benefits of creating and sustaining a relationship versus the costs and benefits of ending it.
- **Knowledge-based trust** occurs when an individual has sufficient information and understanding about another person or organization to be able to confidently predict their future behaviour. The confidence in the prediction stems from repeated interactions, communication and forming a relationship.
- **Identification-based trust** takes place when relationship participants understand and promote one another and can act for each other in interpersonal transactions, sharing core values.

Trust evolves and changes over time. A positive, trusting relationship that develops and matures moves from calculus-based trust to one based on knowledge and, finally, on identification. However, in the case of many commercial relationships, it can also end abruptly at the first calculus-based stage. The relationship with your target audience starts with their initial search and the development of your calculus-based trust activities (this form of trust is based on the financial exchange, of a transaction for goods or services, where the potential loss has to outweigh the estimated gain of the transaction). If you are consistent with your activity and offering then trust is validated. Both parties can then start to acquire a knowledge base about each other's needs, values and priorities. There may on occasion be no further opportunity for the relationship to develop past this point as the transaction may be a one-time-only occurrence. Only a few relationships move to the stage of trust grounded in knowledge and mutual identification, but these are the relationships your brand should strive to achieve and retain by creating and sustaining a passionate, respected and trustworthy brand.

But how can this process be applied to social media brand community activity? Trust can be developed in SMBCs from a number of sources, however not all sources need to be present in all situations. For an organization's social media strategy to be effective and engage with audiences it is important to first be aware of the different trust stages along the purchase journey, as well as the potential engagement activities that can help consumers reach the next phase of trust. In this regard, a broad staged approach to trust can be developed considering initial trust and continual trust.

Initial trust

For the initial trust phase, there are a number of potential bases for trust dependent on the social media site being used. These bases can include 'dispositional trust' as well as rational calculation of required commitment or cost advantages of participation. Dispositional trust is the propensity or tendency to believe in the positive attributes of others in general and is especially important in the initial stages of any relationship. In the early stages of relationship development, consumers rely on their disposition to trust organizations they have not dealt with before because they have little or no specific information by which to judge them. This describes the situation when a consumer explores a new SMBC or unfamiliar website and trusting relationships are just beginning to be established.

For example, when a consumer visits an SMBC for the first time, their initial trust will be based primarily on first perceptions of trust-relevant attributes such as the accuracy of any product/service information that the community displays. Cognition-based trust is active in this stage, and is dependent on quick, cognitive cues, or 'first impressions'. These perceptions are linked to the vanity metrics of social media, such as the size of the community (number of fans/followers), but also include factors such as security and ease of navigation – which means the easier your SMBC is to navigate, the more trustworthy consumers will automatically find it.

The initial trust stage can also be impacted by social stereotyping, which is often defined as a 'mental shortcut' for consumers. Category membership and in-group bias lead consumers to associate positive attributes such as honesty, benevolence, integrity and co-operativeness to other SMBC members as well as the brand's reputation. If individuals feel a sense of belonging for, and also identify with, the brand community as well as fellow members, they can be categorized as brand community members. Within SMBCs, for instance, the interaction of members is often digitally-mediated, where members rarely interact face-to-face but still share a social identity.

In this initial stage, online trust is also based on rational calculation of potential costs and benefits – calculus-based trust. This source of trust is particularly appropriate for SMBCs, which are often rationally motivated at this stage. According to a recent study by Market Track, which surveyed 16 product categories, 80 per cent of respondents said they would do online price comparisons in all categories before making a purchase in a physical location. We previously highlighted how a brand's reputation can impact the initial trust that a consumer will feel towards it – institution-based trust. Formal mechanisms are used to create trust that does not rest on personal characteristics or on past history of exchange; institutional guarantee structures are built into the relationship, such as formal contracts, guarantees and legal recourse available to the consumer in order to ensure success of a transactional exchange.

All of this amounts to building a comfortable, secure environment for consumers so that they are more likely to trust the SMBC. If all of these aspects are in place, the next stage in the journey is 'continual trust'.

Continual trust

Through positive and regular interactions using an SMBC, consumers may move on to the stage of continual trust, which is based on the consumer's knowledge, experience and understanding of the brand based on previous engagement. The process of developing trust relies on consistent interactions and the consumer's evaluation of the brand's activity and evidenced trustworthiness so in this phase factors such as positive interaction, content and familiarity with the SMBC's navigation are vital to reaching this milestone. The later stages of continual trust represent mutual empathy and identification with each other (identification-based trust) and sharing values that the brand represents. If organizations like yours are looking to engage with their target audiences, it is crucial that your strategy considers the relevance of different sources of trust at different stages of trust development and in different contexts.

Let's turn our focus to the main components of consumer-brand trust: credibility, honesty and benevolence. The term 'credibility' is concerned with the knowledge and expertise that businesses possess that is required to complete consumer orders. So credibility refers to the belief that the individual or organization you are dealing with has the ability to carry out the task they claim they can do, such as delivering a product on time. Credibility is dependent on a consumer's belief that a supplier has the required expertise to carry out their role in the transaction effectively, with competence and reliability. In order to gain consumers' trust, your brand should convey the image of a fair and reliable exchange partner, i.e. communication should be targeted and credible to reduce consumer resistance.

Honesty or 'integrity' relates to the belief that the brand the consumer is dealing with keeps its promise about their product or service – for example, the features or capability of a product. And benevolence is the belief that the brand has the consumer's best interests at heart and there is genuine concern for them as a customer. Benevolence is defined as a customer's belief that an organization is interested in their welfare and is applicable within the context of repeated consumer–seller relationships, requiring familiarity and prior interaction between parties. The traditional acceptance of benevolence refers to a supplier acting with good intentions that are beneficial to a buyer. However, in life and when we engage in business transactions we are not always aware that in our minds trust is being built or damaged based on these three components. This can sometimes lead to poor judgement decisions, such as emphasizing one aspect of trust (credibility) while downplaying another (benevolence), often leading to trust being completely undermined. These components are all related, which is something you have to remember when planning your activity. For instance, honesty and benevolence have been found to be highly connected to one another when trust is developing – both components contribute to a general sense of 'warmth' and warmth is something we are programmed to judge very quickly (Kulms and Kopp, 2018).

Considering each of these aspects, digital trust can be defined as the confidence consumers have in a digital platform to protect their information and provide a safe environment for them to purchase products and services and to create and engage with content. Digital brand trust underpins every digital interaction by measuring and quantifying the expectation that a brand is who or what they claim to be and that it will behave in an expected manner. By developing an understanding of the process of building digital trust, you will be able to determine how your brand can perform better on each component as you can build trust on one of these dimensions but still be weak on others. There are actions your brand can undertake to build digital trust through social media engagement, which we will review in detail throughout this book.

Why is trust so hard to gain?

Before we look at trust strategies, let's first consider why digital trust is so hard to gain. With issues such as fake content, the lack of face-to-face interaction, false identities or fabricated SMBCs/websites/email addresses created to trick vulnerable consumers into transactions or even relationships, it is becoming harder to ascertain what is real and what is not (e.g. fake news), what private information is protected and what is open or sold on to unknown parties. Scepticism has certainly risen in recent years, in part fuelled by changing customer expectations; there used to be an acceptance that brands existed to meet the needs of consumers, but that, fundamentally, brands had the power and the customer had to accept what was being offered to them. Nowadays, customers are much more global in their outlook and have lived through recent high-profile examples of mistrust.

For example, consider the recent issues of government surveillance or organizations selling personal data, such as the Cambridge Analytica Facebook political scandal of 2018. Here, it was revealed that Cambridge Analytica, a British political consulting firm which combined data mining, data brokerage and data analysis with strategic communication during the electoral processes, had harvested the personal data of millions of consumers' Facebook profiles without their consent and used it for political purposes.

The scandal has been described as a watershed moment in the public understanding of personal data and resulted in a massive fall in Facebook's stock price and calls for tighter regulation of tech companies' use of data. Incredibly, more than $100 billion was knocked off Facebook's share price in a matter of days and politicians in the US and UK demanded answers from Facebook founder Mark Zuckerberg. The scandal eventually led to Zuckerberg agreeing to testify in front of the United States Congress in a highly publicized event in April 2018. A scandal such as this can quite rightly increase consumer scepticism. Nevertheless, Facebook arguably bounced back. Brands like Facebook can bounce back from high-profile mistakes if they have generated enough consumer goodwill, demonstrated a willingness to resolve the problem and created a sense of belief in the product and service they provide.

If gaining and sustaining trust was easy, then organizations wouldn't feel the need to invest the necessary time and resources to have a truly credible brand. The issue is that consumer values and behaviours are constantly changing and as a result more experiences, both positive and negative, are being shared with wider audiences than ever before. But this is what is so frustrating for some brands: they recognize the need to develop meaningful connections with their customers, but they are just going about it the wrong way. We'll look into emotion later in this book and how effective it can be for engagement but it needs to be followed up with a promise. So many of our decisions are based on emotion but they require a positive result at the end of a decision. Unfortunately, brands often misinterpret that emotion, which is why creating social media communities can help brands move closer to the heart of their audience.

Due to the significant increase in social media users and online socialization, interactions with SMBCs have become part of everyday life for consumers. According to the Global Digital Overview 2019 report from digital agencies 'We are Social' and 'Hootsuite' around 3 billion people, roughly 45 per cent of the world's population, use social media, and we spend on average two hours a day interacting on these platforms. The main reasons people add social media 'checks' into their daily routine are for benefits such as obtaining product, service or social information as well as potential networking possibilities.

A social media community serves two purposes: first, the ability to deliver marketing information to subscribed fans or followers, and second, as an online community where consumers with similar interests in specific brands can share and exchange experiences and information, so it's important to consider that consumer trust in your brand may be based on both information attributes and community attributes displayed within your communities. With that in mind, consider the prospect that your target audience and customer base are positioned within different trust stages along their purchase journey. According to PWC's Global Consumer Insights Survey (2017), more than one in three (35 per cent) of consumers ranked 'trust in the brand' as among their top three reasons for deciding to shop with a retailer. These scenarios reinforce the necessity for your brand to be aware of and act upon the requirements for digital trust, namely the creation of initial trust and continual trust development. If a consumer does not develop initial trust in a brand from their first visit to a social media brand community, there is next to no chance that they will return to the community or visit their website to make a purchase.

SMBCs are also environments for self-expression and can provide emotional experiences for consumers. Not only have participation rates increased recently, but so too has the type and amount of information community members voluntarily disclose. In today's digital arenas most consumers are mindful that social networks can be an attractive avenue for criminals and although consumers are aware of the risks and threats associated with their social media activities, counterintuitively their concerns are not reflected in their actual behaviour. This phenomenon is also known as the 'privacy paradox'. The privacy paradox is a consequence of the competing demand to use information technologies (such as social media) and have an online persona while simultaneously having to guard against potential threats to personal safety and privacy resulting from the misuse of consumers' available information.

General SMBC activity indicates that users often do not hesitate to post photos, share opinions and upload videos in environments that are largely lacking in security standards and practices. This is because consumers tend to trust other community members' expertise, identity and personal information. But they also trust the social platforms to protect their information. In this respect, you might argue that social networking has now reached a stage where there is a predisposed but mostly unwarranted amount of trust. Having said that, it is important that brands remember there are different types of trust that consumers possess, extending beyond just a trust in security offered by the brand. Which raises some key questions for organizations. In an ever-competing marketplace, how can brands stand out from competitors to appear more trustworthy and go the extra distance to increase consumer loyalty? How do SMBCs maintain social capital for brands as well as the interrelationships between trust, social media, social capital and consumer engagement?

Social capital theory

Social capital reflects the relationships and institutions, as well as the social assets of a group that can be used to gain an advantage. The term is often used in sociology, politics and economics, but is also applicable to digital marketing practices. Social capital considers the benefits obtained from social relationships and interactions, such as knowledge sharing and emotional experiences, and can be viewed as a key factor in the success of an SMBC. Some researchers consider trust to be an antecedent of social capital, whereas others consider trust to be an outcome of social capital. This is a bit of a psychological digital version of 'Which came first, the chicken or the egg?' Social capital is a term that has a number of definitions in a number of fields. Overall, it can be considered as an overarching theory that unites concepts such as social networks, trust, social exchange, social resources, embeddedness and social support. When applied to an SMBC, social capital is considered to be the sum of the actual and potential resources embedded within, available through and derived from the network of relationships possessed by an individual consumer.

For SMBCs, the concept of social capital can be considered as a method of displaying the value that can be built up through an online community and from the social resources of the influencers posting and viewing content within that network. Which then leads us to 'embeddedness', arguably one of the most vital concepts of social network theory. Embeddedness refers to the belief that consumers are social beings whose attributes and actions are conditioned by their location within networks of 'concrete, ongoing personal relations' (Granovetter,

1985). Social capital is the result of embeddedness, and considering that embeddedness is a state of mind, the SMBC is the visual representation of embeddedness and social capital is the resources that can be used which benefit the community members. Embeddedness is concerned with the influence of an SMBC on its members' behaviour and can be divided into relational and structural embeddedness. Relational embeddedness focuses on the relational dimension of social capital and describes the relationships people have developed with one another through previous engagement and experiences. Basically, relational embeddedness highlights and reflects the quality and depth of a relationship.

Structural embeddedness looks at the dimensions of social capital and highlights SMBCs' overall structure and concerns the properties of the social system and the network of relations as a whole. Within SMBCs, the relationship between trust and social capital can be analysed on different levels. From a community perspective, social capital can be considered a collective resource that enables productive outcomes such as the exchange of valuable information for consumers with an interest in a brand's products or services. The reason why this is so attractive to brands is that where social capital and trust exist, community members do not need costly monitoring from brands as they can rely on community governance based on informal trust, reciprocity and shared behavioural values. A key aspect of social capital is how we share messages digitally, which involves electronic word of mouth.

Digital social capital, then, is a way for your brand to understand the potential and value of your SMBCs. One of the goals with all your social media activity should be to accumulate more social capital – the more social capital you can create, the more opportunities there are to develop trust. Your brand can gather social capital by developing connections with and endorsements from SMBC members who also have a considerable amount of social capital, such as influencers and partner organizations.

Electronic word of mouth

Most people are familiar with the term 'word of mouth', which reflects how both positive and negative reviews of someone's experiences can be shared verbally. The concept can also be applied to digital platforms when reviewing a brand's products and services, classed as Electronic Word of Mouth (e-WOM). E-WOM can be defined as any positive or negative statement made by potential, existing or previous customers about a product or organization, which is made available to a number of people and institutions via digital channels.

With positive e-WOM enhancing purchase intention, and negative e-WOM reducing it, crucially though, e-WOM influences purchase intention through its impact on consumers' trust.

Trust and e-WOM intention

SMBCs allow consumers the opportunity to obtain information related to products and services concerning a specific brand. The trustworthiness of this information includes various perspectives, such as accuracy, objectivity and reliability. In SMBCs customers' interpersonal trust is deeply embedded in their identification with others and a high level of identification with others in an online brand community would also develop positive e-WOM from consumers.

When consumers trust others and identify themselves as part of a community then they are more willing to spread e-WOM. In addition, a high level of identification-based trust will make customers believe that what others share in a community is of good quality and therefore they are willing to spread e-WOM to their social connections.

Consumers' trust in a brand and their e-WOM intention (their motivation to share positive or negative information in a digital setting) towards a company's products and services has been well established in previous research. The research has argued that a consumer's intention to share information in a digital setting is significantly predicted by motivations such as altruism (selfless concern for the wellbeing of others), egotistical (preoccupied with oneself and the gratification of one's own desires) as well as brand and community-related factors such as brand identification and social trust. The two factors of social media trust, information-based and identification-based, significantly influence brand trust, which in turn influences e-WOM intention.

E-WOM communication depends largely on the connection and trust among people. Information-based trust in social media communities does not directly predict e-WOM intention and this could be due to consumers trusting one specific brand but not trusting other brands that an organization promotes and sells, so they may not convey e-WOM to other consumers. However, trust in a company's social network community can also directly influence users' behavioural intentions towards a brand. Nevertheless, trust transference theory helps in explaining e-WOM intention in social commerce websites, where trust in a close social networking community may be transferred to trust in the companies within their SMBC.

To reiterate, trust in social media activity is comprised of trust in the information (information-based trust) and trust in the members on the site (identification-based trust). Using the trust transference theory, both information-based and identification-based trust in a company's SMBC are good predictors of customers' trust in a company. When consumers have a positive previous experience of an organization, then they tend to depend less on information-based brand page trust to form their brand trust.

Trust is a context-dependent construct, which implies consumers' own experiences provide a more comprehensive understanding of how trust operates in a specific context so your brand may choose to focus on improving and reinforcing information trustworthiness, including its accuracy, validity and objectivity. For instance, regular content and engagement reviews to determine the effectiveness of social media postings and credibility can also be measured through customers who post high-quality information. In addition, since company trust is a key mediator between social commerce trust and e-WOM intention, more product/service information could be posted in your SMBC to improve user perceptions of the integrity, benevolence and competence of your brand.

When customers have a rich prior experience with a company then they tend to depend less on social media community trust constructs to form initial brand trust. Therefore, managers of a social media brand community should potentially focus on customers' level of prior experience. In summary, social media communities have prominent features for driving value for both companies and users. Consumers' trust in the information and in the members of a social media community can result in a stronger sense of trust in a brand and could drive customer intentions to spread e-WOM to their connections. Nevertheless, the impact of e-WOM depends very much on the 'connection strength' that consumers experience within an SMBC.

Connection strength within SMBCs

Historically, connection or tie strength covers a broad spectrum of relationship levels: Granovetter (1973) referred to connection strength as the 'combination of the amount of time, the emotional intensity, the intimacy (mutual confiding), and the reciprocal services which characterize the tie'. This concept is very much a key part of an SMBC. SMBCs are platforms that connect consumers from all different types of backgrounds and social circles. It is due to this variety that the connection or tie strength between community members can vary.

Within SMBCs, connections are created when members interact with one another and subsequently connect themselves to other users and the community. Most social networks promote the formation of new connections, be it with mutual contacts such as the 'people you may know' function on Facebook, or the suggestions of who to follow on Twitter based on followers with similar interests or content, with whom you have engaged.

A significant number of connections within SMBCs like Facebook can be characterized as strong, as much contact within Facebook is between people who are friends, have worked together or see each other in person more or less frequently. In terms of trust, this is more likely to develop among 'strong' connections due to the existing emotional ties and past experiences.

This is not the case for all SMBCs; the majority of ties on LinkedIn, for example, could be described as 'weak', with principles of existing friendship often not applicable. Many online connections are between people who are 'weak' connections, due to their relationship being hampered by social and physical distance, or never having directly worked together, though even second- and third-degree connections can be useful when people are looking for information. Weak connections are related to 'thin' trust, which can be described as a broader but a more abstract form of trust.

E-WOM connection strength

Source/recipient tie strength has been found to impact upon the level of influence associated with a personal information source from e-WOM.

Within online social networks, tie strength or source closeness may be far less relevant as a source of influence. Essentially, the links or ties between a message recipient and all members of their social network should be stronger than the links between a recipient and online community members outside of their social network. Consumers often rely on opinions posted to online feedback systems to make a variety of decisions and in the majority of cases the sources of such opinions are not known at a personal level. The suggestion here is that within a social network 'weak' sources (such as unknown social media members) may be just as influential as 'strong' sources (friends/connections) in driving brand trust.

Because of their greater structural ability to provide new information or novel insights, weak connections can at times provide more useful knowledge than strong ones. Weak connections allow SMBC members the chance to engage and interact with a variety of other users who may not share the same interests. Weak ties are related to sparse networks and loose structures so this suggests that users who are loosely connected within an SMBC can access remote regions within the network and have the possibility to obtain new, non-redundant and innovative information. Weak and strong connections have their positives and negatives regarding the enhancement of the users' social capital. The appropriate type of social capital for SMBC users to embed themselves in is dependent on the users' requirements for information and engagement. Conversely, the influence of structural and relational embeddedness on a brand's SMBC performance depends on the environmental context and the information requirements of the organization. With these different types of connections occurring between consumers within an SMBC a further challenge for your brand is determining when to join their conversations.

Consumers value and trust the opinions they have access to on SMBCs because they regard fellow consumer opinions as genuine and helpful. The issue for organizations keen to participate in consumer conversations is to engage in a way that consumers interpret as genuine and caring rather than another method to hard sell a product or service. As Rick Kauffeld, Principal with PwC US, states: 'Brands have to think about the way for them to engage so that they come off as being authentic and caring and contributing to the network rather than doing something in the self-interest of the brand.' For social media officers the issue of knowing when to join in an online discussion and knowing when to hold back is often difficult. For instance, if your SMBC community allows consumers the option to publish comments/reviews for a product that are factually inaccurate then you should clarify the error while maintaining a positive, friendly image and tone. Your appointed social media representatives must be able to interact and communicate online with sensitivity and diplomacy – including knowing when to participate in an online discussion and when to hold back – while consistently conveying a positive and likeable image.

Brand transparency also encourages e-WOM, which can unfortunately include negative reviews and comments. Previously, brands have been able to hide such comments if they were on their website. However, if there is something wrong with your product or service then it won't take long for customers to voice their frustration on social media. We'll look into how to handle this in more detail when we review reputation management later in the book but fundamentally if you don't have a plan in place to handle such comments then potential and existing customers will soon lose trust in your brand. Nevertheless, just as negative instances can go viral so too can positive ones, particularly for brands willing to own up to their mistake and do everything possible to satisfy customers. Admitting responsibility, recognizing your error and doing what you can to ensure the customer is happy can very quickly turn a customer complainant into a brand advocate.

Brand transparency and consumer trust

Managing your organization's brand identity involves promoting the values, image and endorsers of the brand to your target audience. Understandably, it is an activity that needs to be handled with considerable care and attention. The previous brand approaches afforded all the control of this activity to be with the organization but due to the ever-changing environment of the Internet, companies now include customers in their processes and as such, brand identity management has evolved into a collaborative process.

We've highlighted how consumers are in the pilot's seat these days when it comes to deciding their engagement journey with brands and which destinations or brands to ignore so let's turn our attention to brand transparency and trust. Brand transparency and trust are two vital and connected elements of any successful brand. If there is no trust then it will be extremely difficult to convince your target audience to purchase your product/service over a well-established competitor. Without brand transparency, your customers won't take the risk that comes with giving an unfamiliar organization an opportunity or the benefit of the doubt. In the digital world where consumers can literally block your brand from their timeline, because they don't trust or agree with your values, the key to building trust is showing consumers that you are worth noticing. One of the best ways to do this is to focus on brand transparency. When used effectively, brand transparency and trust can increase sales and profits in a number of ways. Not only does transparency make it easier for you to convert new leads, it also means existing customers will stay loyal to your brand.

If you want your brand to become part of your target audience's daily routine or even their lives, then it is crucial that you share with them everything they need to know about who you are, where you came from, where you are going and what your brand stands for. Consumers want the companies they purchase from to be more human, more engaged and more reliable than ever and that's exactly where your brand transparency begins. In the past it was natural for some organizations to keep certain aspects of their operations hidden from their target audience, such as where their products were manufactured or materials sourced from. However, in today's environment such secrets are no longer acceptable. In order to develop a relationship and build trust your organization must be mindful of providing the customer with full access to each part of your brand's story. Embracing this approach can understandably be difficult and quite frankly embarrassing at times, especially if it means owning up to a mistake but it is also the best way to begin and sometimes repair long-lasting relationships with customers.

This can be a risky strategy, which some brands are reticent to get involved in, as certain revelations about the brand's history or activity could damage the reputation they have worked so long to build. However, consumers are far more understanding than some brands give them credit for and being open and honest about mistakes and poor decisions – as well as being sorry for them – can often cause a positive reaction to a brand. The reality is that if brands want this kind of reputation and have such relationships they have no choice but to be upfront and honest so let's look at some strategic considerations for brand transparency for your organization which can lead to increased trust.

Consider how you promote where your products come from

Your target audience wants to know 'everything' about what they buy. Was it manufactured ethically, for example? Take the case of McDonald's, when customers began to really scrutinize their ingredients and the processes they used to sell food. The fast-food chain faced a huge drop in sales but instead decided to adopt a brand transparency strategy and change its reputation.

McDonald's has launched several campaigns in recent years promoting their healthy menu. Consumers, however, continue to link the brand with unhealthy eating.

'What frustrates us is that when people don't know us, they tend to judge us,' says Kevin Newell, EVP-chief brand and strategy officer for McDonald's USA. 'We're saying don't judge us before you know us, and we're giving you an opportunity to know us like you've never had before.'

What McDonald's realized was that public consumer trust is crucial for their business model. As a result of their transparency campaign, sales began to rise again when customers knew that they could trust what they were eating. Effective packaging and website design remain crucial for sales but you still need to include product background if you want to increase your profit margins. If you don't provide information regarding how your materials are sourced, or what your corporate social responsibility values are, consumers may be less likely to trust your brand.

Show the emotional side of your brand

Whenever you're interacting with customers or thinking about making changes to your business, consider how you can connect with consumers on a deeper, more personal level by showing your human side. For example, if you have a new member in your company, no matter what their position, let your customers know through a social media update that someone has joined your organization who shares your values and the values of your customer. When consumers engage with brands they want to develop a connection. Often they base their purchase decision on emotion rather than logic. As Douglas Van Praet, author of *Unconscious Branding: How Neuroscience Can Empower (and Inspire) Marketing*, highlighted: 'The most startling truth is we don't even think our way to logical solutions. We feel our way to reason. Emotions are the substrate, the base layer of neural circuitry underpinning even rational deliberation. Emotions don't hinder decisions. They constitute the foundation on which they're made.' So, no matter whether your offering is cheaper, more convenient or even just 'cooler' than the offerings of your competitors, your target audience will always go to the brand with whom they feel they have an emotional connection. With effective transparency you can display your values using the people or employees working on promoting those values.

Provide up-to-date and historic company information

Today, your customers and leads can search for any information, and at any time they want, with just a few clicks. If this information is not readily available, alarm bells will start to ring for it begs the question, what have they got to hide? Transparency includes promoting all activity such as annual reports and strategic documents. Though they might not seem glamorous or the most engaging content, they serve to reassure your target audience that you are happy to share all aspects of your organization.

Incorporating brand transparency into your overall brand strategy

Now that we've looked at the initial considerations for brand transparency we can look at incorporating brand transparency into your overall brand strategy to develop trust. Where to start? Being transparent doesn't mean promoting every single detail of your business, such as how often your team takes a coffee break, so you'll need to determine what's important and what your target audience cares about. A good place to start is often the most important question for your customers – the price. Customers don't make their purchase decision purely on cost but they always want to know why they are being asked to pay a certain amount. For example, Apple justify charging higher prices as they promote themselves as a premium innovative brand and highlight new features. Whenever you are promoting your product or service be mindful of highlighting the benefits or features justifying the cost to the consumer. This may not be the right approach for you and it may not be applicable for all industries, so one further strand of transparency that you can consider is providing insight into how your products are made to stand out from your competitors. I've already highlighted how important this approach is to develop trust; how, then, can you promote this on social media? You may decide to have a detailed 'about us' section on your Facebook page, highlighting brand ethics as well as how you are an environmentally conscious organization. Insights such as these help to reassure your customers and target audience that they are engaging with, and purchasing from, a socially responsible and trustworthy brand.

Blogs or information sections on your social channels or website are also great for transparency and you can also utilize video production to reflect your organization's dealings. For instance, you may promote your brand values and state that they are a part of your company's culture, but adding a more human element to this promise by showing staff testimonials or customer feedback through video can help increase trust. Indeed, according to research commissioned by Forbes in 2017, viewers are 95 per cent more likely to remember a call to action after watching a video, compared to 10 per cent when reading it in text format. There is of course a danger that these videos can appear overly-staged and not come across as authentic. This is usually the case when brands are trying too hard, so try and find the right balance between being positive about your organization and being professional.

Staying with the video aspect of transparency, one further approach that more and more brands are using is live streaming. Live streaming has seen significant growth recently, with platforms such as Facebook, Instagram, Snapchat and YouTube all offering this facility. I mentioned earlier the issues you may have with appearing 'authentic', but unlike recorded video, live content is natural and in some cases unpredictable. Consumers are well aware of this danger, so live streaming can portray confidence from your organization, which is passed on to consumers, thereby allowing them to resonate with your brand.

Brand transparency and loyalty

Only after you've developed trust can you begin to cultivate what every brand strives for, which is brand loyalty. Brand transparency and loyalty go hand in hand but it's important to remember that while transparency is crucial to loyalty, you won't see results overnight.

Successful companies have maintained outstanding corporate images by demonstrating consistent values, products and campaigns designed to instil confidence in their target audience. But perhaps most importantly successful organizations are the ones who accept full responsibility for anything positive or negative that occurs as a result of their business decision making. 'The buck stops here' is a phrase made famous by former US President Harry S. Truman, who kept a sign with that phrase on it on his desk in the Oval Office. The phrase refers to the idea that the President has to make the all-important decisions and accept the ultimate responsibility for those decisions. This statement can also be applied to your brand when making a promise to customers. If, for instance, your unique selling proposition (USP) is low pricing or a bespoke unique service, it's up to you and your organization to hold yourselves accountable to the values and standards you have set according to your USP. When creating trust for your brand, a crucial aspect of the process is managing consumer expectations and if you are not meeting those expectations, you need to learn quickly. Customers will often forgive what they perceive is a one-off mistake, but will be less forgiving if such mistakes happen more frequently. If you consistently fail to meet expectations, then your customers will never be able to trust you. In order to instil this approach to your strategy, or review an existing one, you need to determine your vision and purpose that reflect the promises your brand is making to your target audience. Once you have them in place they can be used as an important guide whenever you need to make crucial decisions about your brand.

When determining your vision and purpose, it is important that they are both realistic and achievable. Even the most efficient organizations in the world will make mistakes from time to time, so try not to make promises that for all your best intentions you won't realistically be able to keep. Having aspirations is fantastic and demonstrates you are an ambitious, forward-thinking company, but don't try to convince your audience you'll definitely be the best in the world or that it's impossible for you to make a mistake. Instead, be sure to consistently communicate that if you do make a mistake, you'll be the first to admit it, you'll aim to resolve the issue as soon as possible and emphasize that the buck really does stop with you.

In summary

Following the expansion of online commerce, digital brand trust is crucial for your organization's success due to its increased importance in the eyes of consumers. For any business relationship, brand trust is vital for many reasons.

- Trust creates and develops positive attitudes towards organizations and can lead to customer loyalty. Numerous research studies indicate that brand trust is a critical factor in encouraging purchases over the Internet. Digital brand trust concerns the degree of trust customers experience in online exchanges or through digital platform exchanges. Or more generally, digital trust can be defined as an online user's psychological state of risk acceptance based upon the positive expectations of the intentions or behaviours of a digital brand.
- Creating and maintaining consumer trust through social media is a consistent challenge for any organization. Fundamentally, your brand needs to be authentic – in today's competitive climate, it is what consumers value the most.
- Viral campaigns can be fun and impactful but they may be quickly forgotten when the next trend hits consumers' timelines.
- Regular up-to-date and relevant communication with customers can be a key differentiator for your target audience. We know that authenticity isn't easy but this shouldn't stop your brand striving to be authentic to develop trust. Successful brands provide content that creates value for consumers, which in turn provides transparency and trust.

3

Engagement and Trust

Full disclosure. Consumer engagement is a priority for most brands today but as consumers experience different journeys there is no absolute definition or action plan that is guaranteed to drive engagement. Most organizations would describe consumer engagement differently and if we consider some different perspectives you will be able to see which elements apply to your organization's mission and values. One of the most impactful definitions for consumer engagement was put forward by CRM expert Paul Greenberg of Hubspot (2014) who said, 'Customer engagement is the ongoing interactions between company and customer, offered by the company, chosen by the customer.' Let's review that last part one more time, 'offered by the company, chosen by the customer'. What's great about this statement is that it highlights that the core element of engagement is the consumer actively choosing to interact with a brand and indicates an amount of emotional investment is required for effective engagement to take place.

However, among brand researchers there is a lack of consensus on the engagement concept and definitions vary greatly, from broad, overarching definitions which involve a combination of cognitive aspects (e.g. being interested in a brand's activities) to behavioural aspects (e.g. participation in a company's activities) and/or emotional aspects (e.g. feeling positive about a brand's activities). In terms of an actual scientific definition, academic Dr Linda Hollebeek (2011) proposed that consumer engagement is: 'the level of an individual customer's motivational, brand-related and context-dependent state of mind characterised by specific levels of cognitive, emotional and behavioural activity in direct brand interactions, where the focus lies on the interactions between a specific subject (the customer) and the focal object (brand).' The implication here is that cognitive activity refers to the level of focus or concentration towards a brand, while emotional and behavioural activities represent the level of an individual's pride, inspiration or the level of energy expressed while interacting with a brand.

A common factor among engagement research is that consumer engagement is a psychological process which customers experience in order to become loyal towards a brand, outlining the process by which brand loyalty and trust may be developed for new and existing customers. However, engagement is not just a two-way relationship between brand and consumer, it also involves the interactions of consumers with one another. As long as the topic they are discussing is centred on your brand's activity, this can certainly be classed as consumer engagement. As we'll discuss more, there are different types of engagement that have varying levels of impact and resource required against your campaign objectives or goals. For instance, a Facebook post and YouTube video are both engagement activities, but the promotional video may require considerably more input from an organization. We can say that engagement is the most crucial aspect of social media as organizations strive to obtain a larger share of consumers' attention and engagement with their pages. Nevertheless, social media consumer engagement varies as consumers may spend just minutes or several hours reviewing brand content. The length of time your target audience will spend on your social media channels will depend on their motivations, which vary and effectively encourage different behavioural responses to the content you provide or share.

Purchasing behaviour on the Internet

The Internet provides a number of avenues for online information seeking and the comparison of attributes and prices. As a result, online purchases are influenced by a number of stages in the decision-making process of consumers. The introduction of Web 2.0 (the second stage of the development of the Internet, covering user-generated dynamic content and social media growth) in recent years has brought about additional possibilities for consumers which go beyond product purchase. Consumers can potentially post reviews of products, read reviews by other consumers and exchange experiences concerning products, brands or services. All these aspects feed into the decision-making process in order to resolve a problem, which is comprised of problem recognition, information search, alternative evaluations, purchase decision and post-purchase evaluation. Consequently, tailoring marketing communications to different consumers and knowledge of the buying decision-making process and its determinants are crucial.

There are a number of online shopping benefits which all consumers experience, such as greater access to information, competitive pricing and broader selection. However, despite these benefits the main obstacles to shopping online can be prohibitive – security, privacy concerns and the suitability of the products being sold.

Internet search results are now placing smaller organizations in direct competition with larger brands which means that, faced with an overwhelming number of options available, consumers look to social media to further inform their decision. This provides organizations with the opportunity to distinguish their offering from larger brands while using the same social media platforms.

The classic models of buyer behaviour indicate that the buying process commences with problem recognition and is followed by an information search and evaluation stages, depending on the level of purchase involvement (i.e. cheap or expensive purchases). So once a customer has found a brand that they trust, they will be more likely to re-purchase from the same organization rather than follow the standard re-qualification route suggested by traditional models of buyer behaviour.

In order for businesses to be successful they need to be constantly aware of purchasing behaviour and to monitor consumer attitudes and motives towards the products or services they offer.

Consumer engagement in a social media brand community relies on the quality of information connected to the brand. Consumers within SMBCs perceive information quality as the extent to which the given information meets their expectations but also meets their requirements of the activity they are looking to increase their knowledge of. Having consistent informative and engaging pieces of content provides consumers with positive experiences, which in turn increases their brand connection and eventually, their engagement intentions.

Conversely, if poor or inaccurate information is displayed then this can have a negative impact on the brand, causing frustration for followers. This is of course a key challenge for brands, who seek to provide regular updates with detailed and credible sources of content to allow consumers to become aware or increase their awareness of the brand's offering.

Engagement: Conceptual foundations

Engagement is a combination of cognitive aspects (e.g. being interested in a brand's activities), behavioural aspects (participation in the brand's activities) and/or emotional aspects (feeling positive about a brand's activities). Consumers join SMBCs for a number of reasons, such as to seek information and receive advice, in order to aid their understanding more about the products they use, for entertainment and to reflect their concerns. They also may join following a recommendation from a friend or social network connection. This highlights that the level of engagement is not the same for all people and that the term 'community' does not mean the same to everyone, which is a crucial consideration for your business's activity.

The theoretical roots of consumer engagement can be examined by drawing on service-dominant (S-D) logic (a framework for explaining value creation, through exchange, among different actors put forward by academics Stephen Vargo and Robert Lusch) and relationship marketing theory, which proposes as an organization delivers value to their customers, the strength of their relationship with the customer will improve and increase customer retention.

The S-D logic is a framework that conceptualizes business exchange theory (the exchange between two or more parties of tangible or intangible activity, with rewards and costs involved) by considering service as the main purpose of organizations and attempts to explain how different network actors, such as customers and other stakeholders, can co-create value while interacting with each other. The reasoning behind this theory argues that the co-creation of superior value replaces the more traditional notion of value provision, suggesting that creating superior value in co-operation with a customer becomes a source of competitive advantage for brands. However, the nature of value is highly contextual and is subject to experiences, which suggest that value is achieved using a combination of resources and therefore cannot be created unilaterally, making the customer a co-creator of value. While S-D logic and relationship marketing perspectives highlight customer behaviour as being influenced by interactive and co-creative experiences within complex relational networks such as SMBCs. Social exchange theory can also explain the rationale behind consumers' motivation in contributing to value creation.

Social exchange theory argues that one party will perform a favour for another party with the motivation of an expected equivalent future return.

The Engagement Cycle

When a brand understands the needs of its customers then it is in a position to strategize their approach. One such approach was put forward by academic C.M. Sashi (2012) through a process called the engagement cycle (Figure 2). Sashi defined the engagement cycle as a way of satisfying customers by providing superior value than competitors to build trust and commitment in long-term relationships. SMBCs are able to facilitate this engagement process in an interactive manner and the engagement cycle can be defined in seven stages: connection, interaction, satisfaction, retention, commitment, advocacy and engagement.

1   Connection – Substituting, although not completely replacing, traditional, direct, physical methods are new online methods

Source: Sashi (2012: 261)

FIGURE 2 *The Engagement Cycle*

utilizing social media. This can be more cost-effective and quicker than traditional methods and more global in the potential reach.

2 Interaction – Many organizations have set up and enabled networking and interaction, and in particular have found that they receive a 'push' of information from consumers, as well as a 'pull' from market research activities.

3 Satisfaction – Following on from a successful interaction, it is anticipated that satisfaction results from this interaction. This is comprised of distinct phases, from anticipation of the interaction, to the success of it and the immediate service afterwards.

4 Retention – The key consideration for a brand is determining if satisfaction leads to the retention of a customer. It is likely to, but there have been studies that have shown that despite a positive emotion resulting from the interaction this has not led to consumer loyalty. The emotional perspective here can be unclear.

5 Commitment – This can be calculative (cost-saving) or affective (brand attachment), or convenient or emotional, with each liable to change depending on circumstances. However, a combination of both is likely to produce a stronger commitment and social media may be able to deliver this.

6 Advocacy – Closely related to endorsement from consumers, this is likely to produce either e-WOM advocacy or in the social media age a 'like' on Facebook or 'retweet' on Twitter. It can also encompass advocacy on behalf of consumers from the seller.

7 Engagement – When consumer delight is shared and is combined with loyal purchasing behaviour, the cycle has turned 360 degrees and a customer can be said to be engaged.

A further framework for the consumer engagement process was proposed following a study from Brodie, Hollebeek, Jurić and Ilić (2011) from data collection and analysis of consumer blog posts, represented in Figure 3.

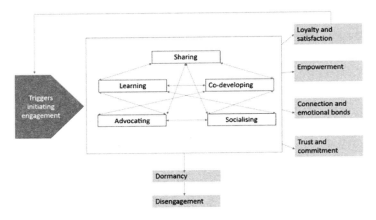

Source: Brodie et al. (2011: 6)

FIGURE 3 *Consumer Engagement Process*

The model shows that consumer engagement is a process that generates consumer loyalty, satisfaction, empowerment, connection, commitment and ultimately, trust. However, the model also indicates that the consumer engagement process may include a transitory state of consumer 'dormancy' and end all engagement (disengagement) with your brand. This is basically where consumers are no longer interested in your community offering and stop engaging with your SMBC.

Whereas trust is developed through sequential stages, this model argues that the consumer engagement process does not follow a sequential progression of phases over time but is formed through a number of relevant sub-processes that the SMBC provides. This is reflected by the bidirectional arrows demonstrating how each area works alongside one another to develop engagement.

The model identifies the five different triggers that consumers experience which can lead to them engaging with an SMBC, such as searching for a product or price information. Other triggers for engaging could also include looking for more information about the company, as well as fellow consumer opinion regarding the brand's products/services.

The triggers then lead to the interplay of five consumer engagement sub-processes:

- **Learning** – The acquisition of cognitive competencies that consumers apply to purchase and consumption decision-making;
- **Sharing** – Disseminating personal details and information, as well as knowledge and experiences through the process of active contributions to the co-creation of knowledge within the SMBC. This represents the behavioural and/or cognitive dimensions of consumer engagement;
- **Advocating** – Consumer engagement expression where consumers proactively endorse and recommend specific brands, products/services and businesses;
- **Socializing** – Interactions which consumers experience to acquire and/or develop attitudes, norms or community language;
- **Co-developing** – Consumers contribute to organizations and their overall performance by helping them develop and test new products, services, brands or brand meanings.

The outcomes of these sub-processes include a number of benefits for brands, such as consumer loyalty and satisfaction, with customers continuing to purchase a brand's offering as a result of their SMBC experience. Due to the open structure and interactive options provided by the SMBC, consumers feel empowered and become actively involved in ongoing discussions and voicing their opinion. There is also often an emotional connection formed as members feel compelled to help fellow members by providing recommendations and guidance, which endorses the host brand. The final benefit that happens as a result of all this engagement activity is increased trust for the brand and its offering.

The engagement cycle and engagement process model are really helpful for your organization as they acknowledge the opportunities provided by

SMBCs to enhance the relationships for your target audience. For your organization to further enhance your brand strategy we can incorporate the level of engagement that consumers may be at during the purchase journey as well as the levels of trust that are connected to the engagement stages. We'll look at a model that combines the trust stages and engagement areas for consumers later in this chapter, but first, let's look at the engagement approaches that brands take when targeting customers as well as the different customer profiles that are active on social media. Considering consumers' engagement motivation, we can now look deeper at their general purchasing behaviour online.

Acquisition and retention

Within commerce there are two basic customer engagement orientations or processes: customer acquisition and customer retention.

A customer acquisition orientation refers to a firm's focus on gaining information about potential customers, measuring their potential value and allocating resources to acquire those with the greatest long-term value. Alternatively, a customer retention orientation focuses on obtaining information about, differentiating between and allocating resources to manage relationships with existing customers on the basis of their long-term value. However, customer acquisition and retention orientations are not mutually exclusive as a business can decide to focus on both to different degrees.

In terms of utilizing social media to acquire and retain customers, there are conflicting opinions regarding the focus and scope of engagement, with some academics emphasizing the psychological state of the consumer, whereas other research has centred on the non-purchase activities of consumers, e.g. posting a positive review which can enhance brand reputation. Nevertheless, when reviewing your social media engagement strategy, it is important to consider the potential impact of each activity you undertake. For instance, simply following a brand on Twitter is a low form of consumer engagement as it requires little processing of the brand meaning. However, a consumer's 'follow' might be viewed by a large circle of followers and even lead to potential followers making a purchase decision.

Effectively, there are two levels of engagement: lower engagement, which describes situations in which people passively consume content or use very basic forms of feedback (e.g. following on Twitter), and higher engagement, where consumers actively incorporate the brand into their lives or participate in various forms of value co-creation, such as blogging or sharing brand posts. Your brand therefore needs to determine its social media strategy based upon the level of engagement that consumers are likely to display and the objectives that your organization would like to achieve.

Lower customer engagement

Organizations of any size can integrate social media with consumer acquisition by running promotions on Facebook or sales offers on Twitter. Consumers with lower levels of engagement might simply consume such information or they may interact with it by 'liking' it or 'sharing' it. These actions can essentially assist brands by creating awareness and influencing other consumers, thereby contributing to the acquisition of customers or prospects. However, activities such as sales offers and competitions do not take full advantage of the interactive characteristics of an SMBC and arguably do not actively engage consumers, which is why these activities are described as lower consumer engagement activities. Although these activities depend on some form of consumer engagement, such as 'liking' a Facebook brand page, they are still limited in terms of the extent to which they encourage consumers to participate in a brand's retention initiatives.

This stage only signifies the first phase of a consumer engaging with a brand. By adopting a 'retention' focus into social media activity, brands can incorporate social media into their efforts to retain existing customers and to enhance relationships with them. For instance, Facebook brand communities have been shown to be effective in influencing brand evaluation among customers who 'like' them. Social media features such as Instagram stories, Facebook Lives and chatbots were created to engage your customers and make them stay with your brand longer. Nevertheless, these features still require effective strategies while using them, as we'll discuss in this chapter, or you may not utilize the main benefits of these tools.

The ability to retain customers is especially important for industries in which organizations cannot easily identify their existing end-customer base, such as fast-moving consumer goods or where brands depend on indirect distribution and could be considered vital for organizations.

A common question asked by brands is 'How do we retain customers if they are difficult to identify in the first place?' This raises the issue that if you don't know who your customer is, then you won't know how to speak to them – or what to say to them. There are three steps that can help alleviate this issue for your brand.

Step 1: Create customer profiles and segments
Utilize all available data sets to collect data, including customer surveys, phone interviews, exit surveys for your website and Google Analytics and create profiles of the type of customer you are looking to acquire and then retain.

Step 2: Conduct primary research

Use the findings from Step 1 to help inform your primary research. Primary research can validate and provide additional insight to how you define your target audience, so focus on understanding who the respondents are and increasing your understanding of the customer journey when they decide to continue to use your brand.

Step 3: Apply this research to your business

Once you've completed your research and know your target audience for retention then you can tailor your content and channel strategy and use your findings to analyse the best methods.

Higher consumer engagement

If consumers are engaged with a brand through their SMBC then a company no longer has full control over the messages to which its consumers are exposed. For instance, consumers with low levels of engagement may simply consume or share brand-approved promotions whereas a highly engaged customer may choose to distribute an independent blog of a company's product or reveal promotional offers that a brand might prefer not to expose to a wider consumer audience. One implication of this phenomenon is that among highly engaged populations, acquisition activities cannot be isolated from retention activities. For example, if a brand chooses to send a specific type of acquisition promotion to prospective customers who meet specific criteria, it cannot rule out the possibility that these individuals will share that information with current clients who do not meet the criteria.

Existing customers may demand to receive the same benefits and threaten to leave an SMBC if it does not comply. A standard strategy for achieving this is to carefully select the customers who receive the message in the first place, i.e. to target customers with a particularly high number of social contacts. However, the inability to separate retention from acquisition represents one of the largest differences between traditional marketing and social media marketing. Within social media marketing such a separation is potentially very difficult for brands since marketing activities are likely to reach prospects and customers of a brand at the same time. This development may potentially cause brands to reconsider the social media techniques that they use for the management of acquisition and retention activities, such as providing new potential customers with more attractive offers which are unavailable to existing customers. Co-ordinating acquisition and retention strategies, as well as multiple social media communities, represents a major challenge for brands in the short term but could potentially improve customer satisfaction, loyalty and profitability in the long term. As highlighted, this can be a difficult proposition for your brand but by analysing the social media customer profiles that you intend to target you can formulate your content strategy to meet the needs of both 'prospects' and 'customers', which we will analyse in the next section.

The effects and reach of a company's social media activities differ among customers and potential new customers, whom we can name as 'prospects'. Prospects have no direct experience with the brand, only a limited interaction with the company, and are therefore more likely to be influenced by indirect experiences, such as news reports in traditional mass media, brand advertisements and brand activities on social media. Unlike prospects, customers' direct experience with a company, its products and brand-related beliefs and attitudes are likely to be held with more confidence and are less likely to change upon exposure to a marketing campaign.

Customer profiles on social media

Both 'prospects' and 'customers' have different antecedents and motives to follow and become engaged in an organization's social media community. For prospects, general company interest or mere curiosity may play an important role in social media engagement whereas for customers, social media communities are also channels for customer service, feedback, industry and company updates.

Customers are therefore in a different relationship stage compared to prospects, which is also reflected in the differences in the antecedents and consequences of social media brand trust for both groups. Customers have more positive perceptions of a company's reputation than prospects, regardless of their intensity of social media use and engagement in a company's social media activities. Customer support via social media could have important side effects for prospects as well as customers, for if they see customers being supported within SMBCs, this may strengthen their perception of the brand. In this regard the conversational human voice is of added value in brand evaluation; the candidness within online dialogues demonstrates enhanced trust and familiarity collectively, influencing the perception by prospects of the organization's corporate reputation. This results in an interesting decision for the brand regarding which type of customer a brand should target through their SMBC. Your brand may be focused with continuously enticing new prospects or may focus on customer retention, as opposed to acquisition, depending on your strategic objectives. It very much depends on your industry, your company history and your existing brand reputation. However, organizations need to continuously explore opportunities to acquire prospects since existing customers may fall away, no matter how intense your focus is on retention. In the short term, firms may not see market performance effects (higher sales or market share) from their social media activities by focusing on prospects. Nevertheless, research carried out as far back as 1954 by Peter Drucker, an iconic management consultant, author and educator, stressed that understanding consumers' changing needs and preferences is critical for companies, highlighting the requirement for your brand to monitor prospects' tastes and preferences for their products and services. Whether you adopt an acquisition or a retention focus or even have the resources to dedicate time to all target audiences, an effective strategy for SMBC engagement and trust is a necessity to achieve your objectives.

SMBC engagement and trust strategy

The strategic engagement roadmap (Figure 4) represents the pathway for a potential brand social media strategy, outlining an objective's focus as well as considerations for how your brand should be positioned and represented through your communities.

Here, your organization should determine the corporate and SMBC objectives, which leads to an awareness review, which in turn influences strategy and ultimately provides value to your brand. The framework also highlights the importance of planning and strategizing the content

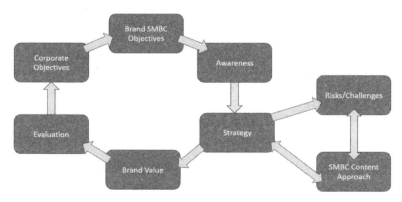

FIGURE 4 *Strategic Engagement Roadmap*

focus for how the brand will engage with customers and set expectations for customer service and engagement as well as the potential risks and challenges associated with SMBC engagement activity.

Considering previous research and industry examples, Figure 5 shows the cognitive, emotional and behavioural aspects of consumer trust which we can then align with engagement activity to form an SMBC Engagement for Initial and Continual Trust Framework to help inform your strategic approach.

Some of the key considerations include:

- **Value Creation** – Information dissemination covering product/ service usage, as well as personal information and experiences between brands and consumers;
- **Credibility-Supplier** – Having the required expertise to carry out their role in the transaction effectively, with competence and reliability;

FIGURE 5 *SMBC Trust Constructs*

- **Reputation** – Attitudinal construct that consists of two components: an emotional (affective) component and a rational (cognitive) component;
- **Incentives** – Financial rewards for purchasing or engaging with an organization;
- **Visuals** – Imagery associated with a social media post which can be subject to consumer interpretation;
- **Security** – Information preserving techniques specifically tailored to social media platforms;
- **Service Delivery** – Act of providing and maintaining a service to consumers.

The level of engagement (i.e. low or high) is also dependent on the consumer trust stage (initial or continual). The staged process framework put forward (Figure 6) highlights consumer digital trust development and key competencies, which enable progression to the next engagement stage. The framework shows that customer engagement is a psychological process that consumers experience in order to become loyal towards a brand, and outlines the process by which brand trust and reputation can be developed for new and existing customers. This accordingly involves

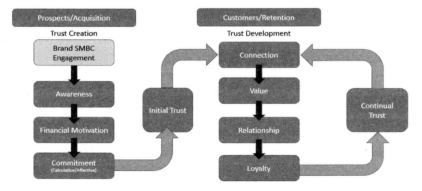

FIGURE 6 *Social Media Consumer Engagement for Initial and Continual Trust Framework*

strategic activities to be conducted at each stage, which emphasizes the need for your brand to utilize industry and consumer knowledge whenever possible. The proposed model represents a seven-stage process, with themes overlapping as initial trust develops further across engagement stages.

To give you a better idea of what these stages look like in terms of activities your brand should undertake, have a look at the table below for strategic activity considerations.

Figure 6 and Table 1 highlight the customer journey and how your brand can develop your social media communication strategies to encourage engagement and develop trust. The framework is based on previous brand research adopting a number of strategies on various platforms as a means of engaging with prospects and existing customers. The concept of a staged approach to trust development, through social media engagement, is generated from a brand's explicit perceptions of their target audience and the content that they find engaging. The framework therefore accommodates a flexible perspective for brands both large and small due to potential resource considerations for some organizations. The requirement for strategic flexibility in your brand's social media approach may prove to be crucial in order to meet your organizational targets and objectives. However, while the process appears sequential for presentation purposes and to aid understanding, trust development involves engagement in numerous social media activities which could occur concurrently.

Achieving customer engagement requires facilitating prospects and customers' transition through several stages in the social media consumer engagement and trust framework. The framework outlines the aspects of initial and continual trust with the levels of engagement connected to prospects and customers. It is important to highlight that social media platforms are consistently developing new capabilities

TABLE 1 *Brand Strategy Considerations*

Customer Stage	Engagement Constructs	Social Media Strategic Options	Trust Stage
Acquisition	Awareness	Watching/listening/observation – Social media monitoring tools, searches	Initial
Acquisition	Financial Motivation	Promotional offers, competition, discounts	Initial
Acquisition	Commitment	Assurance cues, structural	Initial
Retention	Connection	Multiple platform options – Like, follow? Receive regular social media updates	Continual
Retention	Value Creation	Consumer invited to interact/join discussion, questions, opinion (does it come from a person? Call to action within the content to engage, i.e. encourage a response)	Continual
		Asking opinions – interacting with social issues close to the consumer's interest, as well as expressing concern and attention in customer opinions and ideas. Consumers update and change information on their profiles, forward information and share information; consumers respond to the content of others, actively participate, give opinions, but only personally.	
		Negative engagement – organizations should not try to force their way into a conversation.	
		Knowledge – Expert product/industry posts, influencer marketing, video, blogs, social networking, comments.	
Retention	Relationship	A relationship is then formed where co-creation of value exists – Be prepared to reply, bidirectional relationship (the brand knows customer, stands out from competition). Be honest.	Continual
Retention	Loyalty/ Advocacy	Retweets/Posts (e-WOM)	Continual

and while the engagement constructs might still be applicable in the coming years, the technological capability of the platforms could impact the strategies.

The next section goes through the framework stages in more detail using academic insight as well as industry best practice examples to provide you with key takeaways when formulating your engagement strategy.

Awareness

Social media facilitates the establishment of connections between a wide variety of consumers and brands. Social media 'awareness' is a crucial stage in the development of engagement and social media posts should be part of your strategy to find, analyse and engage with consumers.

Customer segmentation

Awareness also requires effective customer segmentation through social media. Social media channels provide a granular way for your brand to identify 'real people' as they allow organizations to refine exactly who they want to advertise to, e.g. males, females, young adults, parents, retirees and so on. The available social platforms allow brands to cross-reference demographics with profile data, behaviour, interests and users' social activity in order to qualify audiences at an intricate level.

This approach has worked wonders for Clinique France, the beauty company who raised product awareness by using the targeting and dynamic creative capabilities of Facebook and Instagram to launch and establish their personalized Clinique iD hydrator. Clinique France's strategy was to develop a highly targeted, multi-phased campaign which took the customer on a journey from awareness to both online and offline sales (Facebook business success, 2019). The campaign was mobile-first, featured short videos with high brand visibility and was developed in conjunction with the brand's agency, DentsuX. The ads focused on highlighting the different benefits of Clinique iD, which effectively delivered the right message to their target audience. The first phase reached 8.7 million women between the ages of 25–45. Which was then followed by a second phase of targeted ads to those women who had watched a Clinique iD video ad or expressed a specific interest in beauty products. The final step was the conversion phase, with the aim to push this audience to the Clinique site, or encourage them to shop offline with offers through dynamic ads. The results were highly successful and according to Facebook business success (2019), between January 9 and February 16, 2019, the company achieved:

- 13-point increase in brand awareness
- 7-point increase in message association
- 20-point increase in ad recall
- 29% increase in 'add to cart' actions

This approach was lauded by Tatiana Lupart, Consumer Engagement Manager at EMEA Clinique: 'This launch was the perfect opportunity to build a data-driven campaign to address the right message to the right consumer. Thanks to the close collaboration between DentsuX and Facebook, the consumer received adapted creatives based on interests and lifestyle. This permitted the creation of customised audiences who received a unique ID combination targeted to their needs.'

As highlighted in this example, segmenting your audience is only the beginning. The rest relies on your brand's ability to define and target audience members by their stages in the trust and engagement framework. The segmentation can then go even further in terms of customers who have interacted with your brand on your SMBC but have not converted and existing customers who have histories of shopping with you but do not engage with your social channels or content.

Identifying and understanding audiences

Commercial success is all about understanding who your audience is and how they behave and interact on social media and then projecting your brand story in a way that resonates deeply with them. Understanding your audience also requires monitoring consumer opinion to develop consumer understanding but it is also important to identify the right platform that matches the characteristics of your brand or those of your target audience. You need to be where your customers 'hang out' with your strategy matching social media platforms to consumer behaviours and social settings – your community environment should mirror a social setting. For example, LinkedIn = a networking conference, Facebook = a coffee shop, Twitter = a festival. Whichever platforms you decide to utilize, the practice should always link back to your organization's objectives. Resource constraints for brands may dictate the platform selection as well as the amount of SMBCs that can be managed – you may feel that your brand needs to be everywhere, but it would be counterproductive to focus time and resource on a channel where your target audience simply don't visit. Snapchat is probably not suitable for a financial accounting software company, so time and energy should then be more narrowly focused on suitable platforms.

These considerations emphasize the importance of a planned approach to measure and evaluate activity and allowing sufficient time to monitor your campaign. Through detailed planning of the use, implementation and measurement of social media, your brand can use SMBCs more effectively and be more confident that the effort expended is worthwhile and effective.

Social ad campaign strategy

For your social ad campaigns to pay off, you need to know your target audience preferences inside and out. For example, this can be as specific as knowing that your audience are males aged 16–25. If you can identify potential customers and understand their lifestyles and purchase habits, you can develop audience personas to help expand the reach of your acquisition strategy. However, be mindful that when brands target all of their potential audiences without considering whether they belong in the prospect or customer categories, they miss out on reaching their most qualified audiences, which decreases the ad campaign's likelihood of producing a solid return on investment (ROI). Although more brands are now becoming more strategic in their approach when segmenting their customers through their CRM database, many still use the same ad for all audiences. As I've highlighted, prospects are consumers who have not previously heard of or have had little interaction with your brand, so campaigns targeting them should focus on introducing your company and the benefits of purchasing from you. If they have clicked on an ad but not purchased, then the ad needs to build on the previous interaction. For instance, with the introduction of Facebook page engagement custom audiences, you can now segment and build audiences based on the interactions people have with your Facebook page and ads. When determining your strategy you can effectively target anyone who has had any form of engagement with your page, which could cover:

- Everyone who has engaged with your page;
- Anyone who has visited your page;

- People who engaged with your post or ad;
- People who clicked on your call-to-action button;
- People who messaged your page;
- People who saved your post (or page).

These custom audiences are best used in the middle of your sales funnel as they target prospects who have previously interacted with your brand on Facebook. However, when it comes to customers who have already purchased from your company before the focus should be on encouraging repeat purchases. For example, a customer who bought winter running apparel may be interested in summer running clothes six months later.

Are you optimizing right?

Prospects and customer groups have different mindsets, so the objective of audience segmentation is to guide your campaign messaging and calls to action. Categorizing each type of audience helps you refine specific messages and make them more relevant in order to resonate with each particular group. Once you have clarity on your messaging, you can apply it to the different groups you can create within your customer database. For example, if you sell a lot of different products then you could segment your audience by product type. Facebook is ideal for such a segmentation strategy as it allows you to integrate your CRM data and target customers across the entire platform. It can also allow you to further refine your prospect matches by excluding customers who might match the search terms but have already purchased from your company. This can be really advantageous for your brand as you will be able to see who you have successfully reached and identify similar consumers who may be interested in your brand's offering. When planning your next campaign, factor in the following considerations to ensure you are effectively segmenting your audience and utilizing your customer database:

- **Keep a list of all active buyers**: Developing and maintaining a list or report of active buyers will ensure that you exclude them from your prospect campaigns. As your social ad campaigns become more successful these exclusions will increase and you can further segment this list for future customer campaigns. If you decide that a campaign will focus on one of your services or products, you may choose to target customers who have made a recent purchase. This tactic is in itself a further segmentation opportunity so you could potentially target customers who purchase monthly or have purchased in the past six months, for example, using special offers to attract their interest and increase their loyalty;

- **Get granular with your data**: If your brand is relatively young, you may not have lots of customer data to analyse but it is beneficial to fully understand how this could assist your segmentation in the future. Alternatively, if you are well established, consider how you can get more out of your data. Your data isn't just advantageous for segmentation, it can also help you create more compelling ads and resonate with each group more effectively. The more successful your brand becomes the more important it is to analyse and consistently review your customer data from several different viewpoints. Each product or combination of products provides you with a further opportunity to segment your audience. Paid social media advertising is a popular tactic for brands which yields positive results but only if brands segment their audiences properly.

Awareness – Key takeaways

Figure 7 outlines a potential framework for your brand to follow when considering your brand awareness through social media activity.

The 'awareness' stage involves your brand becoming visible to consumers. Strategically, organizations are able to do this due to their presence on a number of social media sites, which completes the first stage of customer engagement. If the social platforms match their values and they have the resource, brands can set up a number of different SMBCs, allowing them the opportunity to significantly facilitate consumer interaction with the brand. By developing a comprehensive awareness of consumers' social media brand community activity intentions and behaviours, your brand can utilize these insights in the development and implementation of more effective content in order to attract and retain customers. Having the ability to target exactly who you want and then take elements from your customer database, which include consumer preferences specific to how they interact with your

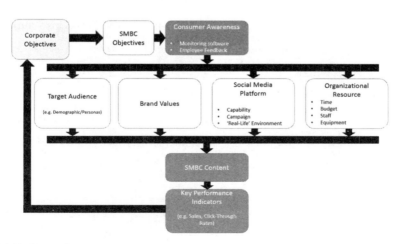

FIGURE 7 *Consumer Awareness*

brand, is an incredibly powerful tool that social advertising possesses. It's about knowing which platforms are going to work for you and you can find that out through statistics and the different demographics that are growing within the different networks.

Financial motivation

Often consumers interact and engage in SMBCs to enter competitions or receive rewards such as discounts. This is classed as an 'exchange relationship', where consumers determine what they give as a 'cost' and what they receive as a 'reward' (Aggarwal, 2004). Within an SMBC setting, brands consider rewards to be the level of financial or psychological appreciation for their proactive existing members or new followers and display the benefits that customers obtain through their engagement with the brand. Providing financial incentives can be a crucial driver for engagement and trust building, particularly in highly competitive industries, as rewards influence consumer behaviour when deciding which SMBCs to join and participate in. Brands should always attempt to create value through their engagement with SMBCs but also aim to provide some financial and/or non-financial rewards to develop and sustain engagement.

SMBCs greatly expedite the opportunity for your brand to promote financial incentives to prospects and customers. Due to the competitive nature of most industries, financial promotions can assist the establishment of connections with a large number and wide variety of consumers. This approach is often undertaken by large brands, which adds support to social capital theory whereby organizations believe that consumers pursue some sort of economic value when engaging with SMBCs. Having a financial motivation focused approach can be key to developing engagement in order to attract and retain target customers. Highlighting your prices and understanding the incentives that customers search for and find appealing is crucial for brands to continue the engagement process. The need for rewarding consumers at this stage can help your brand attract the attention of consumers and develop an understanding of the various reward incentives that encourage consumers to engage with your community. Discounts or deals will always get consumers' attention and it is common to reward consumers for sharing or liking offers on Facebook, or by creating a competition.

Although a common tactic, this approach alone will not continue consumer trust development. If it is easily replicated then it is difficult for brands to stand out from their competitors and encourage loyalty and trust as it can be seen as a quick fix to gain interest but it is not a sustainable strategy for your social media content. Financial incentives have a place in the engagement process as they get people interested in your brand offering, but there needs to be a balance to sustain consumer interest.

Financial motivation – Key takeaways

The relative magnitude of financial incentives for consumers can influence engagement and consumers are certainly motivated to become engaged due to the monetary benefits they receive from the organization. Nevertheless, purely adopting this approach will not sustain engagement and develop trust due to the number of other brands also adopting this approach. Therefore, although financial saving posts get consumers' attention, a variety of content is crucial for trust development.

Commitment

Another key stage in the engagement process is consumer commitment and for consumers there are generally two types of commitment: affective and calculative commitment. Affective commitment concerns the emotional commitment involving trust, whereas calculative commitment is based on rationality, such as lack of choice or cost savings. For instance, a consumer may purchase from a brand due to discount prices, which is linked to financial motivation, and calculative commitment can potentially lead to higher levels of customer loyalty for brands. However, this could not be classed as an effective method to demonstrate commitment because while a consumer may indicate that they were happy with a cost saving, there is no indication that they would not use an alternative store if they were to offer a similar deal.

Affective commitment is more emotionally charged and occurs due to the trust and reciprocity in a brand and consumer relationship. For example, an online consumer who regularly purchases from an organization might develop a personal relationship with an organization's employee, who remembers the consumer's previous orders or interests and provides excellent service. The resulting affective commitment therefore creates higher levels of trust and emotional ties to the brand.

Commitment – Key takeaways

Continued interaction between brands and customers through an SMBC can enable the transition through different stages in the consumer engagement and trust framework. This can then be used by the brand to foster retention and create affective and/or calculative commitment. However, the specific SMBC used for this approach may depend on the nature of the interaction sought, with different SMBCs preferred for different brand objectives. Customer loyalty may be considered the result of calculative commitment to a product, brand or company, while consumer brand trust is the result of affective commitment to a product, brand or company. If consumers are loyal and trust the brand as a result of engagement, both calculative and affective commitment could be achieved in which the consumer and brand sustain a strong relationship. The three main factors for SMBC commitment are consistency, finances and entertainment. By satisfying transactional customers, your organization can attempt to develop stronger relationship bonds and develop continual trust. Commitment is a key indicator of successful engagement, leading prospects to potentially become customers.

Connection

One of the key elements which brings a significant amount of engagement success is the 'experience' that brands create to 'connect' with a consumer, making them the focus of the social media post and establishing a connection with prospects. In order to develop a connection with prospects and enhance your connection with customers, your organization needs to establish what encourages them to connect with your SMBC and feel secure enough to trust your brand. This tests the capabilities of your brand in terms of demonstrating your enthusiasm, commitment and concern to the customer through engaging and emotional content.

Employee connection

Consumers often experience the candid way that staff from organizations respond with a conversational human voice to several types of online feedback such as questions, compliments and complaints. In previous research from van Noort and Willemsen (2011), conversational human voice has been shown to be of added value for brand evaluation and candidness in online dialogues enhances trust and familiarity. One way to achieve this is never to underestimate the effectiveness of personal signatures or names added to the end of SMBC responses. This approach makes consumers feel as though they are dealing with an actual person, not just a faceless corporation. It also shows them that the organization is willing to take personal responsibility for the transaction or issue and not hide behind a generic brand signature.

While being enthusiastic and personal are important attributes for connection, the most important is the ability to provide accurate and up-to-date information. This is crucial as brands on social media could be accused of focusing on profitability and not the needs of the consumer, yet personal relationships can certainly assist your overall performance. Not only must staff running your SMBC be knowledgeable, or have quick access to those in the organization who can respond to technical enquiries, they must also be afforded a degree of trust from the company's owner/manager to react and respond to a customer in a manner that positively reflects your brand. Even if it is just a holding message, stating their enquiry is being investigated, an open and honest response which indicates a time frame for an answer goes a long way towards developing trust.

Connection – Key takeaways

To ensure your target audience is reached, your brand should identify methods to connect with prospects and post content that is centred on engaging with them and making them feel that they are in a safe environment. You can develop this connection with prospects by creating

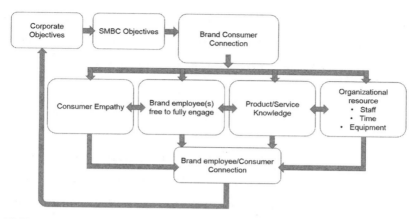

FIGURE 8 *Brand Consumer Connection*

content close to the consumer's interest as well as expressing concern, attention and attempting to inspire them. From your brand's perspective, the importance of understanding how consumers engage in SMBCs and the consequences of this connection is vital. Your brand needs to listen to consumers and continuously interact with them in SMBC communications.

Developing a consumer connection is crucial for building trust. Connection activities or indicators highlight the need for consumer empathy, and highly knowledgeable staff with a freedom to engage as they see fit, as well as sufficient resource, are needed to carry out this activity. These practices are conceptualized in Figure 8 and begin the next stage of engagement: creating value.

Value creation

The concept of value co-creation stresses that the value of a service or a product is not created solely by a brand but mutually created by an organization and consumer of the product or service. The need for interaction by instigating discussions and sharing content is crucial for the next stage of trust and consumer engagement. Many tactics exist to provide value to consumers who engage with brands through social media, however some of the most effective content for value creation comes from user-generated content (UGC).

Social media is filled with user-generated content, which is content created by consumers that is publicly available, readily distributable, possesses some degree of creativity and is not constructed through professional content creation practices. UGC produces social 'currency' for marketers as it helps define a brand, while social media provides endless avenues for communicating – it is the consumers who serve as the influencers, not the technology. Academics Markus Zinnbauer and Tobias Honer (2011) continued research into this area and described social currency as a process whereby consumers recommend a brand or share information about a brand. Their research suggested that social currencies are derived from interactions between consumers and are usually beyond the direct control of a brand. Through their empirical study Zinnbauer and Honer proposed that there are six components of social currency, which are detailed in Table 2.

Although social currency consists of six different components, as detailed below, brands do not rely on them all to facilitate brand loyalty among users. The average consumer wants to feel a real human connection to your brand before agreeing to engage and purchase from your company. Consumers scroll through their social and digital news feeds on their devices to be entertained and to research new and interesting content. If the content is rich and creative enough to capture their attention, they're more likely to click on your offers or promotions; customers who have positive experiences with your brand are then motivated to inform friends, family and colleagues by sharing their experiences. Referrals are one of the most effective and cheapest ways to increase your customer base. UGC provides authentic information

TABLE 2 *The Six Components of Social Currency*

Component	Brand Context
Affiliation	The value of a brand is closely linked to the affiliation and sense of community it creates among other like-minded consumers. Brands create value by promoting the community and building exchange opportunities.
Conversation	Prospects or customers may proactively discuss a brand's products and services with each other. By engaging in these conversations, brands can instigate further conversations and discussions by providing additional knowledge and perspectives.
Utility	Social exchange with other consumers provides an opportunity for brands to build invaluable utility for customers or consumers by helping them to increase their own social relevance.
Advocacy	Prospects or customers are willing to tell others about a brand or recommend it further. This brand advocacy is one of the key value drivers.
Identity	Prospects or customers develop a strong sense of identity and the ability to express themselves to others by using the brand.
Information	The more information prospects or customers have about a brand's products or services, the more likely they are to develop preferences for that brand.

about the brand's products and services from previous customers which enhances your brand credibility. For instance, with an average of 60 million images uploaded to Instagram daily, UGC is among the most popular and scalable ways for brands to showcase products, praise fans and drive revenue through social media today. Providing information connected to the industry, which is of interest to the consumer and hence motivate them to continue to visit the SMBC, is also a key strategic method as it highlights 'shared motives'. Value Creation can also be demonstrated not only in the desire to understand more about potential products and services but also in relation to key news and information concerning the industry.

Further value creation factors can also include product knowledge searching as well as a sense of belonging to a community. However, these motivational factors may not be the same for organizations who decide to become engaged in social media. Again, this reinforces that from a strategic social media point of view your brand's goals in social media should be linked to your general operational objectives. Consumer engagement through a SMBC should focus on consumers' interests and needs in order to provide superior value that is relative to competitor activity. This can potentially be achieved by creating, disseminating and responding to intelligence regarding consumer needs in keeping with preferences and seeks to develop trust and commitment in relationships with customers.

At this stage of engagement and trust development, your brand should also provide consumers with commenting opportunities. The commenting opportunity will help your organization identify and reach consumers more easily, watch their reaction and gauge their opinion. At the value-creation stage you can also identify consumers who have established relationships with your brand and on the basis of their experience produce and share content through your social media. These consumers are motivated to communicate their personal goals through self-expression and at this stage consumer loyalty to the brand and trust is developing, therefore it is important to offer platforms where engaging discussions take place, which are capable of attracting further potential fans of the brand. Although SMBCs demonstrate high levels of engagement and loyalty to a brand, the activities of such platforms can also have a negative impact on brand trust so your organization should consistently observe how engaged consumers communicate with one another and seek to enter the conversation when appropriate. Value creation is vital for any effective engagement approach so let's take a look at some strategic options and key examples.

Encourage customers to join the product development process

Major global brands are already taking co-creation of value very seriously in terms of how they develop new products. Starbucks is a prime example, launching a platform in 2008 for this exact reason called 'My Starbucks Idea'. The platform was created to engage customers and encourage them to provide ideas and share their Starbucks experience. In the space of 12 months, customers provided an incredible 88,000 ideas and suggestions to Starbucks. Through the My Starbucks Idea platform, the brand gives customers and other stakeholders a voice in refining the company's future business model, as well as a prominent role in the creation of new products. Treating customers essentially like partners allows brands further opportunities to promote innovation, new product development and new ideas through mutual collaboration. Similar to Starbucks, in 2001 Procter & Gamble launched the Connect + Develop innovation platform, which empowers customers to post product development recommendations, as well as completely new ideas for products.

When provided with the opportunity to collaborate with your organization customers are more likely to feel more invested in your brand. When your customers are actively involved in product innovation, creation and development it can increase sales and build loyalty. By collating customer feedback and ideas on how to improve your offering, you will have access to data on the latest customer wants and needs that ordinarily you would have to invest resource or funds in order to access this information. Using stakeholder research can also reduce product development costs so adopting a mentality of 'we know best' might be an extremely narrow-minded and costly view for your brand to take.

Enhance the customer experience to elevate your brand reputation

Value co-creation through social media can lead to improved brand management and increased customer value. The value that your brand offers builds on previous experiences as consumers are keener than ever to share their experiences when interacting with brands. Earlier, we discussed how online platforms can be used to create value on the basis of product/service recommendations but they can also be used to improve the customer experience. Computer giant Dell use this method through their platform Idea Storm, launched in 2007, which has implemented recommendations from the platform to form part of their current customer service strategy. As a result of this platform's success, Dell launched a Social Media Listening Command Centre in 2010, which aims to improve customer service and technical support by engaging with customers. A positive customer experience is a critical component of brand reputation. Examples such as Dell demonstrate that brands can use value co-creation to improve transparency, engagement and customer service. Improving the customer service experience ensures your brand receives a boost in reputation.

Enhanced relationships lead to brand trust and brand social media communities can engender value creation practices, where consumers are able to develop close relationships and draw values from their long-term interactions. Social media platforms with virtual touch points also allow brands the opportunity to integrate resources and co-create value through relationships, facilitate user-generated contents and enrich the purchase experience.

To develop value co-creation, brands have to consistently demonstrate their values every day by engaging their communities with interesting content. Organizations looking to create value should provide genuine interaction with consumers online, instigating and participating in positive, honest and inspiring conversations. They should focus on the quality of the content shared on their social media communities, with each post providing value – a fundamental part of the story the brand is telling to its community. This allows your brand an authentic opportunity to share brand messages through creative dialogue.

Put your customers in the spotlight

This is a really straightforward way of taking full advantage of UGC. Clothing brands, for instance, often share posts of customers wearing their products. If you have a dedicated fan base who are posting photos or videos of themselves wearing, using or enjoying your product online, take advantage of this and share through your SMBC. Making UGC work for your brand is not limited to just clothing brands, however. GoPro, the versatile action camera company, produces robust video cameras and software to capture thrill-seeking experiences and regularly shares customer content. High-octane activities like skydiving or snowboarding show just how effective GoPro's products are so the brand looks to share customer videos whenever possible. Such behaviour by brands effectively encourages more UGC as showcasing customer videos provides GoPro with inspirational content, which is likely to encourage more purchases as social media users often search for UGC before making big purchase decisions.

Nevertheless as the growth of UGC presents a fantastic opportunity for your brand it can also come with certain challenges. Whilst there is potentially a lot of content out there that your customers are sharing you must also be aware that consumers are fully aware of their legal rights as content creators, particularly when it comes to copyright issues. Previously, using someone else's videos or photos generally required getting consent from the person who created the original content before it could then be used for promotional activity. Today, with such easy access to digital content through social media, the lines of ownership could be described as having been distorted by brands, publications and other people.

In order to respect consumers' intellectual property rights and comply with legislation, your organization needs to obtain the proper permissions from the content's owner prior to using it for any marketing purposes. Industry analyst Susan Etlinger also reviewed the ethics associated with permission requests in her 2016 paper, 'The Impact of Digital Content: Opportunities and Risks of Creating and Sharing Information Online', and stated that 'when seeking permission to use content, organizations must be honest with the user about when and how the content will be used, and whether it will be syndicated to other publishers or organizations'.

When it comes to digital rights management (a systematic approach to copyright protection for digital media) and user-generated content, there are two vital areas for your brand to consider; implied consent and explicit consent. Implied consent is often linked to brand hashtag campaigns, where the content creator has included a branded hashtag along with their image. Often brands will state their terms and conditions for uploading an image with a specific branded hashtag on their digital channels, making reference to the usage of the image for commercial activity. The issue with this form of permission is that you can't be certain that the user has seen or read the terms and conditions, therefore the permission is only implied. Explicit permission involves the brand contacting the content creator to state exactly what they intend to use their content for and not acting upon those intentions until they have received permission to do so. As UGC becomes even more valuable to both consumers and brands, your organization should seek to obtain explicit consent, to make it easier for your brand to use this type of content across all of your marketing channels. Successfully implementing UGC consent requests as part of your strategy, means your brand can considerably reduce legal risk and protect your brand reputation.

Include UGC in your promotional competitions

A really quick way to generate UGC is to ask your followers and customers to submit their content as part of a competition or giveaway by your company. This strategy was utilized by RYU, a Vancouver-based athletic clothing retailer, who in 2017 launched a campaign through their Instagram account entitled #WhatsInYourBag. The aim was to promote their products with a giveaway by encouraging customers to share photos of the RYU products they had in their own gym bags and incentivized them by offering prizes. The campaign generated thousands of posts and helped increase their overall social media following. Just to flag up that with any UGC it's important to state in the terms and conditions that content may be used for other promotional purposes once it has been submitted. Including a giveaway as part of a campaign is an effective way to engage your target audience and raise awareness of your brand. UGC that is competition-based can also give your brand increased exposure if the winner is decided by a poll as the entrant will be motivated to share their content as much as possible.

Integrate fan photos and videos in your advertising campaigns

UGC can contribute massively to building and maintaining a loyal customer fan base, particularly when you share customers' content as part of your marketing campaigns. For instance, the Disney 'Share Your Ears' campaign in 2018 focused on raising money for the Make-a-Wish Foundation so encouraged customers to share photos of themselves, friends and family wearing Mickey Mouse ears through social media using the #ShareYourEars hashtag. For every participant, Disney pledged a \$5 donation to the Make-a-Wish Foundation with a \$1 million cap. However, because customers loved the campaign idea as well as what the funds went towards, Disney eventually had to double its original pledge to \$2 million to give to the charity.

Brands need to consistently assess and review UGC to completely understand its influence. Traditional marketing now co-exists with Consumer Generated Advertising (CGA) and as a consequence, online retailers need to be aware of CGA as it can positively support traditional marketing or may negatively impact and undermine it. CGA differs from firm-generated advertising (FGA) because each type of advertising (CGA or FGA) generates different discussion content for an advert. Consumers tend to display appreciation for FGA but CGA can be more entertaining, causing consumers to discuss an advert more. Research conducted by Taylor et al. (2012) which investigated Self-Enhancement as a Motivation for Sharing Online Advertising found that consumers trust CGA over FGA and the more entertaining an advert or post, the more it will be shared. Social media users' message-sharing behaviours could also be attributed to the need for self-enhancement. When consumers view a message or post on social media from a brand they perceive to be consistent with their identity, they are more likely to disseminate it among their social contacts if it reflects who they are and what they are interested in. In short, your brand should consider the symbolic and self-expression properties of your online ads and match them to targeted consumers' self-concepts.

Value – Social media incentives and visuals

Adding a visual element to any post increases its visibility on consumers' social media timelines, as well as the opportunity to develop trust. The difficulty for brands is understanding which images will get the most engagement (e.g. likes, comments, shares and retweets) so it may be the case that creating visual content requires trial and error, as well as creativity. Figure 9 shows that visual social media trust is divided into two main constructs. First, the 'brand product' image/video, which concerns the product/service being used. And second, the 'brand image/video' connected to further triggers to develop trust, such as sales incentives and emotion.

Images that incorporate and embody emotion can also be used to engage with consumers, such as inspiration and humour (in keeping with the 'value' construct) in order to inspire consumers to create a trusting connection with the brand. Often the product being promoted is the focal point of the posted image and the main emphasis is to create situations in the mind of the consumer of how the product would impact their

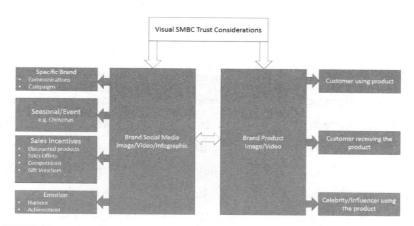

FIGURE 9 *Visual SMBC Trust Considerations*

life, such as the consumer using the product, receiving the product or inspirationally, seeing a celebrity endorsing the product.

This section highlights the importance of images and their variation dependant on the type of post in developing trust. While this is a popular method, it is also beneficial for brands to consider the subjective nature of images and the potential difficulties of controlling the effect or impact of an image or video. For these instances, the visual can be subject to consumer interpretation, which may not seem attractive for a brand wanting to retain control of its reputation. The crux of this matter requires the organization to have a strong understanding of the audience and fully consider how an image may be interpreted by its current and targeted consumers and how it affects their brand reputation. Engaging pictures allow both brands as well as their consumers the possibility to create interesting images for their online social networks, as well as reassuring consumers that they can trust the brand. So, let's look at some examples which have incorporated creativity and visuals into their SMBC strategy.

Social marketing examples

To gain further insight into this area we can look at how some established brands have got creative with their engagement strategy through social media. At this stage the most important lesson is that whether you have a budget of hundreds or hundreds of thousands, creative and authentic social media engagement can help grow your brand.

If your brand operates in a competitive industry, it's vital that you do all you can to stand out from the crowd. This is the situation for Peel, a mobile phone case company that is up against some formidable rivals in a highly competitive industry. Most case brands buy in bulk from manufacturing conglomerate Alibaba and then resell the product for a marked-up fee. Breaking away from conventional practices always gets you noticed and this is exactly what Peel did. Peel sells thin phone cases, their USP being that they are both stylish and functional, so their social media channels are perfect to showcase their products. Peel use Facebook video ads to showcase their story and let their audience know that as a brand they are different to their competitors. Their ad campaigns have been highly effective, with their sales increasing on the back of this approach, and according to the Biddyco social advertising case study, it has worked wonders for them, as they've managed to increase their revenue 16 times and achieve a 3x higher ROI in 2017. So try to focus on creative and innovative ways to set your brand apart on social media, especially in a competitive industry through social advertising.

Another great example of incorporating visuals into your engagement strategy comes from online retailer, Wayfair. The brand is known for selling quality furniture at affordable prices and for a long time one of their main challenges, when using Instagram, was encouraging followers to move from simply looking at a photo through their SMBC to going to their website and making a purchase. This changed in 2017 when Instagram rolled out its new shopping features. By using Instagram shopping, brands are able to 'tag' specific products within a picture so that if consumers are interested or want to know more about the product they can go directly to a landing page and purchase it. The process is so effective because it is a seamless transition for the user, but it also takes into consideration the customer mindset when visualizing how the product looks on its own and also how it looks in its natural environment, e.g. a bedroom or living room. This approach has been successful for Wayfair as they only share content that is going to highlight the benefits of their products and how they can become part of your life.

It's crucial that your brand provides customers with a straightforward shopping experience from a social media search all the way through to checkout. You can achieve this by creating content that is appropriate for the platform you're using, which is also easy to process and lets the customer visualize how the product or service will look when they are using it.

A UGC strategy encourages engagement, but also makes it easy for your biggest advocates to show their appreciation of your brand to their audience. The campaign #AsSeenOnMe by retail brand ASOS is a perfect example of incorporating UGC into an engaging campaign. Here, the brand requested followers use this hashtag when posting pictures showing off their latest outfit from the retailer through individual social channels. ASOS would then share the posts through their official channels. Now this wasn't exactly an innovative tactic but in the caption the brand would include a description of the product as well as a product number. This made it easy for consumers to search for products if they were interested in buying them, so be mindful to always include a branded hashtag so that you can track your UGC campaigns, which can lead to organic engagement and increased sales.

The examples highlighted so far are for brands that could be perceived as being social media friendly, but what if your organization sells products or services that consumers generally feel uncomfortable purchasing or sharing? This could be the situation for TENA's customers, who provide products that help manage urinary incontinence, leakage and bladder weakness. Consumers are usually happy to share pictures of their new running shoes but are not exactly forthcoming when it comes to sharing incontinence products! This is obviously a challenge for TENA but their approach is to highlight just how common the condition is and also provide support to customers. One such campaign in 2018 involved promoting their app 'My Pelvic Floor Fitness' so they developed an info video social media contest. The message was to unite women around an issue many of them experience but few feel comfortable enough to discuss, even with friends. By normalizing such issues and highlighting how their product can help solve them, the brand encouraged their target audience to feel that their SMBC was a safe environment to share experiences. The competition also encouraged customers to engage with one another by posting selfies while doing the exercises which the app promoted. As with any successful campaign, the 'engagement ask' was fun, inclusive and could be done easily. So even if your brand or organization isn't perceived to be 'social media friendly', don't be put off using social media and use it as a method to unite your audience and encourage a safe environment for them to interact.

An important part of your engagement strategy is not to be afraid to experiment. This was the case for Blenders Eyewear, a sunglasses brand which has grown considerably, thanks to effective Facebook ads and Instagram influencer marketing. The company has tried a number of social media marketing tactics to go from selling small amounts of sunglasses to a successful brand with hundreds of thousands of followers. The Facebook strategy that they focused on in 2017 let their audience do the talking for them. Their ads highlighted positive customer reviews and comments about their products, so by combining feedback as well as visible engagement, the ads provided enough social proof to entice consumers to click and subsequently purchase products. The new approach resulted in them achieving a higher click-through rate (CTR), but also decreased their cost per click (CPC). However, the brand's success wasn't just through clever Facebook advertising – their Instagram feed is filled with customers wearing their products. Again, similar to fashion retailer ASOS, Blenders' approach is to develop relationships with satisfied customers.

Aim to incorporate social proof into your Facebook ads to entice viewers to click and develop relationships with non-traditional influencers. Some ways in which digital branding allows organizations to interact with consumers include digital banner ads on certain sites, or creating a video to showcase products and services. With competition fiercer than ever in most sectors, it's crucial that organizations have something that sets them apart (a USP – Unique Selling Proposition) and helps position your brand.

Value – Knowledge

Another key aspect of value co-creation is knowledge sharing. This approach reinforces engagement themes such as education and emotional connection and is crucial in terms of reward, which ties in with affective commitment. It also supports your brand's credibility and being recognized as a source of information is also critical for engagement. Providing industry insights and product knowledge is a good indicator that, like your target audience, you are passionate about the industry that you are commercially connected to. With some organizations this varies, though. For example, it might be as detailed as a technical video showing the correct application of skiing equipment, or something straightforward as their opinion on a football team's line-up. Opinion blogs can also be very effective as they say to customers that your brand actively enjoys discussing industry issues and opinions and if consumers trust your advice, they will trust your brand. However, just because a brand provides guidance in the form of a blog, there may still be some scepticism. Essentially, guidance is just an opinion – you have brands who are telling consumers what to do or what they think are the best options when they produce blogs, but there's still a large element of trust as the blogs may just be showcasing their products' capabilities. This can lead to consumers questioning brand blog impartiality. One way of combatting these doubts is to encourage guest bloggers. Impartiality is a big thing for consumer trust and by showcasing an external person's opinion and reputation, brands can become knowledge hubs by association. Alternatively, brands can utilize influencer marketing strategies.

Influencers

Promoting products via social media influencers can be categorized as a form of subconscious marketing, but how can this trend be explained through psychology? The term 'Influencer Marketing' is relatively new but it is becoming increasingly prominent with brands, with more organizations investing large amounts of their marketing budget on multifaceted influencer campaigns. On the whole this is a worthwhile venture for brands as according to the 2019 Influencer Benchmark Report on average for every dollar spent on influencer marketing, marketers saw an average of $5.20 in earned media value returned. The report also found that Influencer marketing has continued to grow as an industry over recent years. Growth for the market continued to $4.6 billion in 2018 and it is expected to continue its upward trajectory in 2019 to potentially become a $6.5 billion industry.

As you can appreciate, brands are extremely keen on being connected with popular social media personalities. Such is the demand nowadays that an entire industry has been created off the back of the phenomenon, with newly formed intermediary agencies acting as matchmakers between brands and their desired influencers. But how exactly do brands target these influencers and more importantly, how do they spot them in the first place? Well, they don't have any hidden superhuman qualities, unlike Meta Humans or X-Men (comic book superhero references for all those looking puzzled) and they are just normal, everyday people. What sets them apart is that they have a passion they are devoted to and they truly love telling people how devoted they are. This passion can be applied to anything, such as extreme sports, fashion, cooking or video gaming. It's highly likely that whatever industry you are in or whatever products you sell, there will be a passionate influencer out there in the digital landscape. By sharing their passion through social media, these influencers have gathered huge followings and have gained significant online popularity. This has enabled them to considerably influence consumer opinion on subject areas using videos, pictures, blog posts and comments.

It's not difficult to see how this makes influencers an ideal marketing tool for brands. Already they have a large following at their disposal (perhaps significantly more followers than your social channels combined), which can easily be reached by sending out a message endorsed by a popular individual whose opinion they value. The thinking behind this method is that in relaying a message to a group of influencers, they will then positively endorse and promote the message to their huge communities. In return, influencers are financially rewarded or given free products for their part in such campaigns.

But why are these influencers so influential? We've discussed who influencers are and why they are so prominent in digital marketing, but why does their opinion matter so much more than others? Previously, we highlighted how trust and consumer behaviour is closely linked to cognitive reactions and the way in which consumers are affected by influencer marketing is no exception to the theory.

A primary objective should be to develop connections with key influencers that are likely to help utilize the value of networking, find solutions to specific organizational issues and provide additional strategic benefits. Building relationships through SMBCs involves the ability to identify individuals in these roles and to understand and implement the type of approaches to which they will respond. For instance, if you are a B2B, it may be most effective to initiate an online dialogue through a business network such as LinkedIn or suggest a phone call to explore potential ways your organizations can help each other. Or if you are a B2C, you might provide some free products or services to key influencers in return for an objective and unbiased review to hopefully generate positive publicity. Developing a trusted expert or key influencer approach within a particular field could also increase your followers. In all instances the main objective should be to establish trust between parties, which is founded on the ability to communicate in ways that show mutual respect and can be developed over time if the relationship continues.

Influencers – Credibility and social proof

Previous research indicates that the credibility of an endorser is dependent on factors which include trust, expertise, similarity and attractiveness. The level of influence an individual possesses depends on their degree of perceived power. One of the key elements of 'power' lies in perceived expertise so if an influencer is known for discussing and promoting a specific product – let's say snowboards – then they will be perceived to have more authority on that product than an influencer who discusses snowboarding and ski equipment in general. A position of authority is further reinforced by the sheer size of a following. If an influencer has a huge number of followers or their content has a vast amount of likes and shares then this will provide consumers with a form of social proof to affect their opinion. The idea that so many other consumers trust and value the influencer's opinion and recommendations confirms to viewers that their opinion should be valued, the basic premise being that if everyone is doing it, then it must be right.

There is also the tactic of making your product or service look as attractive as possible, which is often the approach for brands that use celebrity endorsements or models using their products. Adding an aspect of glamour also makes your product look appealing (e.g. Hollywood's George Clooney mulling over something cool and interesting while drinking a Nespresso). This is also known as 'attractiveness bias' and as humans, we are extremely susceptible to this. Subconsciously, we often perceive cool, good-looking and charming individuals as having a lot of qualities simply because of how they look and act, which can also lead to positive associations between the individual and the brand. This strategy is the basic concept for clothes models in shops, on posters or billboards: we see healthy, good-looking individuals wearing clothes and think we can replicate that look ourselves. These 'attractive' individuals, opinions and visuals influence the subconscious of the consumer, potentially influencing them when faced with a product-related purchase decision.

Relatability and the millennial crowd

Ironically, the main thing that sets social media influencers apart is that they are just like you and me. Their relatability is what appeals most to everyday consumers as despite having the same level of following as global stars, the stories they share and the tone of content they produce gives the perception of normal, everyday people. Their blogs, vlogs or posts cover everyday life situations and they make a conscious effort to regularly engage directly with followers. Also, their relatability is firmly rooted in being part of the same age group and sharing the same interests as their target audience. Relatability links in with social identity theory, which outlines that people are attracted to the idea of belonging to a group of similar individuals and form part of their own identity as a result of being part of that group. Most social media influencers belong to the younger side of the millennial age range (incredibly, if you were born in 1982, you are still classed as a millennial), a demographic that is historically extremely difficult to reach for marketers. Millennials place a strong emphasis on forming their identity so having role models that are relatable and easy to identify with makes it all the more likely that they will be influenced by their endorsements.

This approach sounds like it has no potential drawbacks or pitfalls but it's important to remember how savvy consumers are. When something sounds too good to be true or someone is being over-the-top in their praise we often develop a feeling that the message may be agenda-driven and insincere so to keep on top of this there are some factors that you must consider when using influencer marketing.

First, authenticity is vital for your influencer campaign. Consider practical questions such as does their personality match our brand values, or would they use our product as part of their daily routine? It's crucial that you take a measured approach and take your time when identifying an influencer who is a great fit for your brand. Only then will your message resonate with your target audience.

Influencer marketing has always had its challenges when it comes to consumer scepticism. Consumers know that brands are rewarding influencers somehow without the individual openly admitting that they are being paid to promote a product, for example so it's important to be open and honest about the relationship rather than risk a negative brand perception by denying all knowledge of such an agreement. Trust is vital for influencer marketing and as we've highlighted, transparency is key when it comes to establishing trust. The number one factor that will promote loyalty for your brand is transparency and that is exactly what your target audience will be on the lookout for when engaging with influencers on social media. This trust concern can be alleviated by including a brief intro in a blog covering product features, which highlights the relationship with the brand, or adding hashtags such as #sponsored or #ad. In all likelihood this will reduce any feelings of animosity towards the brand and increase consumer trust by believing that the content is genuine and honest.

Is influencer marketing right for your brand?

As we've reviewed, influencer marketing has many benefits for brands but this does not mean that the approach will work for all industries. When it comes to social media engagement, there is always the potential downside of user passivity. The passivity of a user is a measure of how difficult it is for other users to influence them, an algorithm which takes into account the passivity of all the people influenced by a user when determining the user's influence. So, to be influential online, not only do you have to be popular, you must be able to convince your followers to spread the message through their networks. This can be very difficult as most social media users are happy to scroll through your content and may even 'like' it, but inspiring consumers to share or comment on content is a challenge, no matter which influencer is endorsing it. So, try not to fixate on your campaign going viral or the number of new followers your influencer has generated. Instead, look at quality over quantity. There may be one influencer you are attracted to who has a huge following over another potential influencer target, but always keep in mind which influencer will be the best fit for your target audience to help you stay true to your brand values. This part of the value stage of the consumer engagement and trust process is founded on consumers' need for information whereby 'knowledge' of the consumer engagement process is highly interactive, experiential and based on aspects such as 'learning', 'sharing', 'advocating' and 'co-developing'. A knowledge emphasis can be advantageous for your brand and seeks to establish and maintain consumer engagement and trust on social media. A knowledge focus can look at providing consumers with detailed product and industry knowledge and recognition as a source of information can also be seen as a reward for consumers being a member of your community. To take advantage of this, your organization should look to provide regular 'knowledge' posts as part of your SMBC content.

Value – Key takeaways

Value creation is based on information dissemination covering product/ service usage, as well as personal information and experiences between brands and consumers. Essentially, value is created through two sub-constructs – knowledge and experience – from both the brand and consumer, which together comprise value creation. These constructs are conceptualized in Figure 10.

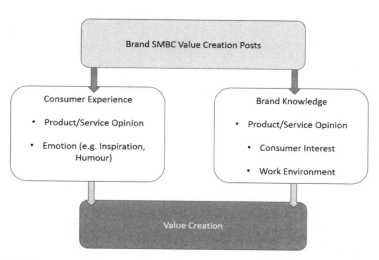

FIGURE 10 *Brand SMBC Value*

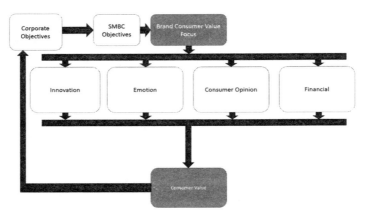

FIGURE 11 *Consumer Value*

Social media platforms facilitate the process of information dissemination and that repeated interaction through long-term relationships is introduced as key to building trust. Value creation involves a strategic consumer focus as well as innovative techniques from brands to stand out from competitors and develop continual trust, as conceptualized in Figure 11.

Remember, the nature of value is highly contextual and subject to experiences so value is achieved using a combination of resources and, therefore, cannot be created unilaterally, making the customer a co-creator of value. Once your customers are confident that being a member of your SMBC will consistently provide value, they begin to form a strong relationship with your brand.

Relationship

A pioneering example of brand consumer relationships is that of Red Bull. When we hear about the brand 'Red Bull', we think of so much more than just their flagship energy drink. We also think of all their supporting activities, such as the extreme sports, music and entertainment they are involved with. That is all down to the promotional activities the organization developed through their own media outlet and Red Bull is now a global brand for sporting activities and action shots, with users following them on social media for their adrenaline-filled content. Posts don't directly promote the product, but rather focus on being informative and motivational so they are committed to offering quality material about a topic of interest. Red Bull is getting closer to their audiences and identifying the best moment and need for their product and fans love these unexpected conversations. Being involved in so many activities, the brand also takes the opportunity to create separate accounts in order to send out content that is relevant to their audience. They have accounts for their racing, biking, gaming and eSports communities and by tailoring content, they have managed to attract a strong fan base who are happy to promote the brand, forming strong relationships with their target audience.

Social media consumer engagement requires the establishment of trust and commitment in brand and consumer relationships. Once the previous stages have been achieved by your brand, an engaging, trusting relationship is formed with customers. At this stage of the engagement process, if a consumer is developing trust in your brand then they can potentially become advocates at a later stage of the process. Therefore, in order to prolong and enhance this relationship, your business should look to strengthen the emotional bonds that have been created, which relates back to the argument that affective commitment establishes and sustains trust in a relationship. But this relationship can only continue if there is consistent satisfaction as well as an emotional bond given out by your brand, such as consumer concern. Concern for consumers is reflected in terms of recommendations in the form of product suitability (for a particular situation) and value for money. If your brand is able to make continuous efforts in these areas and retains a strong customer focus then you are able to differentiate yourselves from competitors. Successful brands which make concerted efforts to listen and act upon customer feedback further cement this positive relationship, encouraging consumers to continue to engage with their brand. The sub-relationship themes are represented in Figure 12 (below).

Incorporating emotion into consumer engagement content can be a successful approach for your SMBC as it can also lead to consumer recommendations as they are excited by the content your brand produces. This approach works because you are tapping into something deeper that comes right back to what we discussed in the branding section in Chapter 1, which is about being remarkable and producing content that people want to share and they want to remark upon too. However, the main pitfall with this approach is to ensure that the emotive content is suitable for your brand or industry, which also relates to the profile of your target audience. The brands that are successful with this method are the ones that delve into psychological desires, where there's some basic human cognitive psychological concepts or behaviourally economic concepts which appeal to consumers. The ideal scenario is for your brand to be the wallpaper in

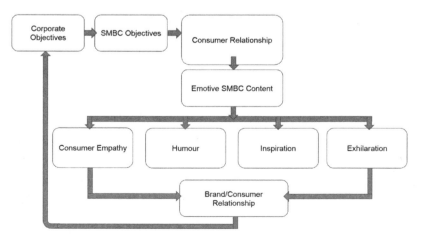

FIGURE 12 *Consumer Relationship*

your customers' lives, but not wallpaper because that's bland, wallpaper because they think your brand is cool, they'll just have it everywhere, and it's part of their life.

Loyalty/Advocacy

The following stage is 'Loyalty' whereby consumers are now fully engaged with an organization and become advocates for the brand. This is where delighted consumers engage in e-WOM to spread knowledge regarding positive experiences with a product, brand or company. Brand loyalty is a deeply-held commitment to re-buy or re-patronize an organization's preferred product/services consistently in the future.

This definition can then be applied to SMBCs, where SMBC loyalty is determined by consumers' opinion of the content provided and the motivation to continue to visit, engage and then purchase the brand's product or service. In order to build competitive advantage, organizations continually look for new, exciting ways to increase brand loyalty among their target audience. Furthermore, engagement provides emotional and rewarding experiences, such as peer recognition, kinship or humour, which can increase consumer loyalty. In order to preserve these feelings or relationships, consumers will consistently visit SMBCs that continue to provide these experiences.

This stage is simplified even more on social media, where a delighted customer can easily tell their social world about the brand's offering and their satisfaction. Engagement can also be increased by favourable brand associations that motivate consumers to share, comment or even produce information related to the brand. If organizations notice such consumers successfully participating in brand communication, they will encourage, motivate and trust them – i.e. will actively seek to engage them in communication in social media and then this will 'foster' advocates of the brand. As well as customers, brands can also play advocacy roles in relationships. This should then hopefully develop into a strong relationship where the brand and consumers look after each other's interests and the focus will be on the exchange of values that transcend their self-interest.

Each brand striving to appropriately enhance brand trust through communication in social media should gradually engage consumers in communication and encourage observers to become active, loyal and advocating consumers. Take, for instance, Innocent Drinks, the smoothie brand who have a great approach to interacting with audiences online. They are always quick to reply but keep the conversation light-hearted and very much on-brand, which has resulted in a fan base of devoted followers who regularly post pictures of Innocent through their own accounts and engage in conversations on numerous topics which aren't always product-related.

Just like brand transparency, consumer engagement is linked with brand loyalty. Loyal customers actively choose to continue engaging with your company because of how your brand makes them feel and how they feel as a result of engaging with your brand. This engagement can be identified by a number of actions from a customer such as purchases, sharing on social media and e-WOM referrals. Each of these actions indicates that a customer wants to be connected to your brand as you share the same values. A general belief among brands is that co-creation of value helps ensure that organizations remain competitive in highly competitive environments. Coca-Cola, for instance, takes advantage of social media platforms by customizing its products and crucially staying relevant to their target audience. For one particular campaign the brand generated a lot of interest when it decided to place customer names alongside its iconic logo, encouraging people to 'share a Coke' with the people they care about. The 2014 summer marketing campaign was one of the most successful in Coca-Cola's history, with incredible results on their social channels, with 988 million Twitter impressions, 235,000 tweets from fans using the #ShareCoke hashtag and over 730,000 glass bottles personalized by customers on the Coca-Cola online Web store.

For your organization it might be argued that your best salespeople aren't actually on the payroll. This isn't meant to cause offence to any salespeople reading this book, but some of your organization's most effective sellers are the ones who have bought your product or service. But crucially the ability to convert them into effective advocates or ambassadors for your brand comes down to the customer engagement strategies you decide to undertake. Thanks to the increased prominence of online reviews, your existing customers' ability to influence new customers' trust and subsequent buying purchase decisions has risen dramatically.

Promoting your reviews on social media

With such a potentially huge audience on social media, successful brands understandably like to share their reviews and accomplishments through the SMBCs. Sharing reviews or testimonials which heap praise on your company's offering is a really effective way of building trust and engaging with your target audience. Your organization may be doing this already but there are a number of factors to consider to really get the most out of your review posts. First, always thank the customer for their feedback (both positive and negative). This would seem a given as it is just a common courtesy but surprisingly, many brands don't do this. By acknowledging their comments, and thanking customers publicly, you are showing your target audience that you welcome feedback. This can then motivate other customers to leave a review when prompted, as they know that you care about what they think of your products or services. A customized response is always preferable if you have the time and resource, but even global brands such as Virgin make a point of personalizing each response and signing their response with the employee name or initials. This level of personalization makes your customers feel that they have a relationship with your brand and encourages them to engage with positive comments in the future.

This can be extended further with your company engaging with customers' social media accounts. You don't want to be intrusive but it is beneficial to monitor what your audience is saying about your brand on social media as consumers will use these channels to share what they feel about your company. If your customers tag or mention you with supportive comments or videos showcasing the best aspects of your brand then these are definitely worth sharing through your official channels. Particularly if the comments are from influential accounts within the media or your industry. Again, if your target audience sees that you share customer comments officially and in some instances to a larger following than they have, this will encourage them to start talking positively about your brand as well in the hope that their posts are then shared. Remember, the review you share will be competing with other posts on a cluttered timeline so highlight any key quotes that come from a review. If customers are intrigued, they can read the entire review but generic posts such as 'another satisfied customer' are unlikely to grab their attention.

Another way to ensure your posts jump out on a customer's social timeline is to include an image. We've already highlighted the importance of imagery for trust development and with so many posts competing for attention, it is always a challenge for brands to stand out on customers' social feeds. A strong positive image can make a huge difference, so look to use a photo of the product or service. If the customer has posted a photo as part of their endorsement, even better. There is also the potential to create a personalized image saying thank you, which the customer may in turn share. While it is important to showcase the effectiveness and quality of your offering, it's just as important not to show off too much. If an SMBC is focused on self-promotion then audiences soon become disengaged. No organization is 100 per cent perfect, so don't claim to be and be mindful that customers are following your SMBCs to learn about your offering and be educated or entertained. Promoting positive endorsement is highly effective when developing trust, but just ensure you maintain a balance when sharing content.

Depending on the size or history of your brand the amount of reviews you receive each week on social media may vary. If you are only ever receiving a few, share them straightaway. However, if you are receiving hundreds or even thousands of reviews, it can be difficult to identify which ones to share through your official channels. While making these decisions, consider which reviews highlight the benefits to the customer when using your brand. The review needs be useful for your target audience and showcase the benefits of choosing your organization so ask yourself questions when going through the reviews, such as does it inspire confidence that products are delivered on time? Or even is the product value for money? If they tick these boxes for example then consumers are more likely to trust your brand will deliver on its promise. This then backs up any Unique Selling Propositions (USPs) that you advertise your company is capable of delivering on.

Try not to fall into the trap of sharing reviews which maybe go over the top when proclaiming how happy they are with your service – e.g. 'I love this brand more than life itself.' Although they might be genuine, consumers may be sceptical at how overly effusive they are and may become concerned that they are fake reviews, which can damage your reputation. It's a fine line between genuine and grandiose praise which can be subjective so perhaps review these comments with colleagues to decide whether or not to share them.

Loyalty: Key takeaways

Loyalty to an SMBC can be defined as the consumer's intention to continue using the SMBC in the future, to recommend it to other users and continue to purchase products from that organization. Consumers' loyalty towards a brand occurs when the consumer's relative attitude towards the SMBC is favourable and in addition there is repeat usage behaviour. Innovative campaigns like the 'Share a Coke' campaign mentioned earlier in this chapter create a buzz that can develop and increase brand loyalty. If an organization is willing to put your name alongside their brand logo then that shows how customer-focused they really are. These campaigns can also generate a lot of publicity as you are placing customers in the spotlight on your social media channels.

In digital commerce customer loyalty is usually lower than in traditional environments as consumers may follow a wide range of SMBCs with different information and products/services from which to choose and with just one click they can change from one SMBC to another. The focus of consumer loyalty and advocacy is dependent on customers becoming an advocate of the content or service (i.e. sharing brand links or positive e-WOM) or actively engaging with content on the SMBC by posting or commenting. The advocacy stage is where a satisfied customer tells their 'social world' about the brand's offering and their satisfaction in using them. Engagement can also be motivated by favourable brand associations that encourage consumers to share, comment or even produce information related to the organization. Nevertheless, your brand must strive to continually provide effective service delivery to encourage this type of advocacy but must be wary that consumer content preferences can vary and therefore not base its social media activity solely on this approach. Showing emotion humanizes your brand and consumers buy from people. When brands post content that resonates with their target audience or creates an emotional reaction, consumers are more likely to want to share that feeling with family and friends. We've all been there where we've scrolled through our timeline and seen a post that is funny or inspirational and thought, my friends will love this, I'll share it. If the content is powerful enough, we often feel compelled to share that experience or cause that we feel passionate about with the people who matter most in our lives.

When formulating your strategy, it's important to take a holistic approach to your engagement strategy. Your customers are complicated individuals and a one-size-fits-all approach to creating and sharing content just won't work. It's not as simple as posting funny memes, videos or interesting content. Consider how the content will make your target audience feel and if it will cause a favourable emotional reaction.

Summary

The analysis is based on academic and industry case study research reviewing strategic social media engagement constructs which create initial and continual consumer trust. The frameworks argue that engaged consumers can become advocates and collaborate with your brand in the value creation process which can effectively satisfy the needs of your target audience. Social media consumer engagement can also entice customers due to the creation of emotional ties in relational exchanges with them. Your SMBC strategy must consider 'awareness' on the part of the consumer. The issue of awareness concerns continuous review of consumer discussion on social media (needs, interests, etc.), but also an awareness of how effective and engaging your content is on your social platforms. Financial motivation and providing value are also key considerations for your organization to encourage consumer commitment to remaining engaged with your SMBC.

Building on from these stages, consistently providing knowledge leads to consumer satisfaction, relationship building and eventually loyalty in the form of advocacy. Access round the clock to your SMBC's media empowers consumers when interacting with your organization and to avoid potential negative trust effects of such empowerment, your brands should encourage and facilitate conversations and not disrupt them. The ever-changing and complex social media environment means that your organization should plan your SMBC investments with care. Your company must understand the area of business they want to address, formulate measurable goals, objectives and corresponding metrics before deciding which social media platforms are most suitable to leverage these.

Before entering into the social media environment, you should have an awareness of what is being said about your brand as this can help confirm appropriate goals and may inform the timing of entry into a particular environment. Effective SMBCs require a long-term investment and brands should focus on consumer relationships and be prepared to participate in dialogue and open conversation, developing effective relationships with customers to ensure trust. Social media measurement is in many ways subjective and potentially unique to the interpretation of the entity doing the measuring. When evaluating the benefits, the focus on financial returns must not be lost, although the benefits associated with intangible conversation and participation can also lead to future returns.

4

The Corporate Value of Social Media

We've already discussed the value social media brand communities provide consumers with engaging content and emotional connections but what about the corporate value your SMBCs provide to your brand? Corporate value from social media activity relates to the return on investment (ROI) brands receive when utilizing SMBCs, such as increasing their audience to acquire and retain customers, enhancing their reputation, increasing their connection with consumers by providing additional customer service contacts and ultimately, increasing sales. The value a brand experiences by using SMBCs involves six themes which are dependent on the organization's resources and aligned with their objectives.

A comprehensive planning process is crucial to the success of an SMBC, if it is to result in a positive ROI. An effective SMBC strategy should not only address the objectives for SMBC use, such as engaging with customers and developing trust, but also how a brand will measure the economic value and business benefits. The focus of any organization should be the corporate objectives that need to be achieved and which SMBCs with corresponding metrics are best to achieve them. The six key areas reflecting SMBC corporate value for brands are:

- objectives;
- audience;
- reputation;
- sale;
- customer services;
- evaluation.

Objectives

Having clear social media objectives helps brands focus on the content they provide and encourages their users to share in order to achieve their overall corporate objectives. The obvious endgame is selling a product or a service but the question brands have to ask themselves is how much they trust social media to help them meet their corporate objectives. For instance, some brands are adamant that all social posts must link directly to their retail site. That's probably the extreme end of a company's social media guidelines but it still indicates that some brands are purely focused on sales and not interested in developing relationships through social media.

Key Performance Indicators (KPIs)

When analysing the value of social media activity, it is crucial to determine your Key Performance Indicators (KPIs) at an early stage. Usually this will involve digital metrics which are relevant to the organization (e.g. click-through rates of posts) so that brands can analyse how much traffic goes through to their website on a certain day or with a certain Facebook post or tweet. Or some organizations are more focused on increasing awareness so may concentrate on the number of mentions they receive, reviews, returns or potentially repeat purchase as a result of SMBC activity. However, there remains some scepticism that social media content still has a long way to go before it can compete with email revenue streams and brands need to trust that their audience will understand the motives for the types of post they share on their SMBCs. Some brands might just want to get hits on their website so having a link to it is perfectly fine whereas others trust their audience will think this is cool content and somewhere down the line this will impact their decision to purchase from that brand.

Nevertheless, social media is extremely valuable when it becomes a predictable indicator of future earnings and potential growth. While investment and results in social media are often cyclical, as with any other marketing campaign, passionate community members can potentially be predictable in their social activity across communities. Social media activity that is frequently measured, such as number of retweets, is meaningful within the context of those people. Therefore social media engagement strategies that are holistic, consistent and focused on your brand's target audience provide value by keeping the brand relevant and extending its reach to other potential consumers.

Platform-specific Key Performance Indicators

One further consideration for brands is that key performance indicators have to match the platforms which are potentially different for each channel, i.e. objectives for Instagram activity may differ from those for Twitter. This depends entirely on the KPIs and objectives of the brand and which business results they want to achieve so there is no correct answer here – and each channel requires a different approach based on objectives and outcomes.

Another consideration for a brand's objectives should include a process of passing social feedback to the correct department or contact to ensure that the feedback can positively impact the organization's strategy. This aspect can frustrate and fascinate organizations in equal measure when using SMBCs as there's a whole load of valuable information to be used if they connect with people properly and they use that information to put the pieces of the consumer experience jigsaw together.

In order to successfully utilize feedback through SMBCs, brands need clear objectives that they can turn to again and again, to then turn around and see how well they've performed. Internal communication can be an issue for some organizations and in some instances the left hand doesn't know what the right hand is doing. Social media responsibility could be delegated to just one individual and that person might be answering ten complaints about the same thing. The customer is quite happy with the response, and that it gets resolved, but if the person or team running that social media account doesn't report the problem to the management team or to the product development team, then you are missing out on valuable feedback or oblivious to an issue that could occur again in the future.

Content frequency

Frequency and timing considerations are also a key consideration for brands' SMBC objectives. Such considerations are applicable to all industries. Say, for example, you're aiming to market products to sports enthusiasts, you have to think about what kind of information they would be interested in reading and what would be the best time of the day to post on their timeline. Successful brands will have content strategies in place which align with product launches or seasonal promotions. However, it is vital that these plans are flexible enough to incorporate ad hoc activity. Again, the approach is very much dependent on the resources available to the brand. There's no point in a brand thinking 'We've got to post five times a day' if they don't have the resources to do so. It's better to do a little, but to do so consistently and over a long period of time.

Audience

Utilizing social media to increase consumer audience requires an established analysis process in place as well as protocols regarding the interpretation and use of that data. Regarding the reach of a brand's social media activity, it could be argued that the higher your intensity of social media use, the more likely consumers will become a 'friend' or 'follower' of your organization and become engaged with your social media content. This signifies the importance of establishing a well-thought-out brand presence on social media. If a social media platform is that popular, followers will post content that they think their fellow consumers will be interested in, which in a way could be doing a brand's job for them. Most firms see increasing their following as a means of expanding the reach of their products and services and with the numbers involved, this can potentially happen but from a community value point of view you're also increasing the dynamic innovative content that could be posted on the community, which will always be a key benefit for an SMBC.

Social media analysis

Many social media brand communities are established with the main aim of facilitating conversations between consumers and the brand. Due to the sheer volume of conversations or mentions that can take place on social media, organizations need to have processes in place which can find and monitor these discussions. Generally, these posts are of an ephemeral nature, without any obligation to respond. Processes such as analysing previous Twitter mentions require an archive system, whereas industry blogs are less about staying connected synchronously and more about facilitating rich, often lengthy conversations, which can be traced back to the blog itself. Traditionally, organizations wanting to address operations have adopted a more quantifiable approach using metrics that have tended to be volume driven, such as number of followers, traffic driven to the website, click-throughs, time spent online, postings and comments, conversions and units sold.

Volume-oriented metrics are valuable to brands and brands that create social communities naturally want to understand what they are getting in return. However, relied on by themselves, they can foster a quantity-over-quality mentality and may not provide the required insight that organizations need to fully understand consumer activity. Social media can therefore deliver other returns with meaningful and measurable financial value. Once a brand has identified appropriate metrics to analyse reputation through social media engagement, an appropriate evaluation tool must be selected. This could either be based on objective data (e.g. number of views or followers) or reviewing sentiment evident from the community postings.

Reputation

Your corporate reputation can be classed as the collective representation of your past behaviour and outcomes that depict your ability to deliver valued results to all stakeholders. Your reputation is a key consideration in the supplier selection process and consumers are more likely to select companies with a positive corporate reputation and are willing to pay more for their products. Furthermore, a positive corporate reputation can protect your company in times of crisis, foster customer loyalty and retention for organizations of all sizes and enable your company to attract more customers. Essentially, reputation is about how trust between parties is developed, assessed and maintained and social media can have a significant impact upon a brand's reputation. Managing reputational risk is the next aspect of social media value for brands to be aware of. In this respect, risk is linked to a lack of understanding of your target audience, failing to display a consistent approach, not keeping content up to date, as well as legal blunders.

Corporate reputation is a valuable intangible asset for brands; however, it is increasingly difficult to manage within social media. Nevertheless, organizations continue to create online communities in the belief that they can be beneficial to a firm's reputation. The implications of this could be that companies lose their dominance over information flows as they are exposed to critics and negative e-WOM, which could affect their brand reputation at a significant speed.

One of the main risks is the potential of adopting the wrong strategy, i.e. one that does not resonate with your target audience. Fundamentally misunderstanding your audience and forgetting to put the audience's interests and passions ahead of your own can be a huge mistake. For example, some brands just want to make a video, which is often quite dull and corporate, and somehow wave a magic wand and make it go viral. Social media approached in such terms is always doomed to fail.

The risk leads to potentially not understanding the capabilities of the SMBC that a brand has chosen to host their community. Brands need to have a good understanding of whichever platform they use because if they don't understand their followers or their likes, all they will do is annoy consumers – which makes them come across as being insincere and lacking credibility. This aspect links into the risk or consideration of posting content which is not current or relevant to the target audience. Often organizations force their brand into something that they think is going to be culturally relevant and it comes across as really cheesy and corny. Consumers don't appreciate that – on the whole, it has to be relevant to resonate with them.

In order for an SMBC to be seen as an information hub, content postings must be relevant and up to date. If that's not the case, brands run the risk of consumers visiting competitor SMBCs to find product or industry updates.

The risk of no social media policy or established process in place for staff is also a concern for brands. In the era of social media, brand staff 'voice' can be a valuable resource, due to their product knowledge or passion for the brand but it can also be a significant risk for organizations as employees who have traditionally had limited choices in voicing their on-the-job experiences can now communicate with hundreds – even thousands – of people outside the organization with a few keystrokes. For example, staff often have their work social accounts connected to their personal mobiles, which in some instances has led to a posting from the wrong account. There is also the factor of human error to consider. Under these circumstances, effective brand management of employee 'voice' in the social media era is crucial for SMBC successful engagement. This can be accomplished by the establishment of an appropriate organizational context, communication mechanisms appropriate for each purpose of voice, support and guidelines that enable employees to make appropriate voice-related decisions supporting the desired brand image and engagement in what employees are saying.

In today's digital environment your brand reputation is more important and more permanent than ever. Whenever we need to buy something new or need further information on a product or service we invariably place our trust in search results, so the importance of maintaining and managing your digital brand reputation increases. Social media comments, posts, images and reviews all impact consumers' search results, but the ramifications of these results are not limited to Google: they affect consumer behaviour, decision-making and above all your organization's brand reputation. Your reputation defines your organization so whatever is connected to your brand in a digital environment will leave an impression on your target audience. In short, your news feed changes all the time but your digital brand reputation footprint will never completely disappear. With all this in mind, it is crucial that you understand how to manage your brand reputation in the digital world.

Hiding away from social media platforms is no longer an option if you wish to actively manage your brand reputation online. Channels such as Facebook, LinkedIn and Twitter have developed from simple forums and now function as search engines, in and of themselves. Consumers use these channels not only to interact but to access information and make purchase decisions, so engaging with social media now means so much more than just having a dedicated page. Most, if not all, companies want to be seen as having a cool reputation on social media. However, a study by social media software and consultancy firm Sprout Social in 2017 found that consumers aren't looking to buy from brands that are 'cool' on social media; instead they are looking to buy from brands that are responsive to them. The company studied 289,000 public social media profiles and surveyed more than 1,000 consumers and found that nearly half of their respondents (48 per cent) wanted to purchase from brands that were responsive. This supports one of the basic recommendations of social media marketing: the conversations you have with your audience are key. Their findings also highlighted some of the key areas that consumers are interested in when evaluating their purchase decisions through the social content they view, which also included:

- offering promotions;
- providing educational content;
- sharing interesting visuals;
- humour;
- exclusive content;
- criticizing rival brands.

Interestingly, the study found several things that brands do that their audience actively dislikes, which includes making fun of customers, talking politics and using slang terminology. Understandably, audience preferences on the personality a brand projects on social media depend on the channel being used. For instance, Sprout Social found that 79 per cent of Millennials (generally classified as those born between 1981 and 1996) and 84 per cent of other generations prefer brands to let their personalities and reputation develop on Facebook. This naturally can be linked to the way content is posted on different platforms. When brands use Twitter, they need to be succinct and link to other types of content, while on Facebook, there aren't the same character limitations and audiences can review most of the content directly on the platform. In today's competitive environment, consumers are less forgiving when it comes to SMBC activity that they don't agree with. The research indicated that 51 per cent of respondents will automatically unfollow a brand that does something they dislike, while 27 per cent block them or report them as spam. Just over a quarter (27 per cent) go so far as to boycott the brand entirely.

Reputation perception on social media

When evaluating the reputation considerations for prospects and customers, it is important to highlight the different antecedents and motives for following a brand's social media activities. Prospects may simply have a general interest. In contrast, SMBCs for customers can provide product/company updates and customer service channels. Existing customers who have a personal experience of a brand are more involved with it and know more about it, resulting from information-seeking behaviour before a purchase (to collect product information) and also after a purchase (to reduce cognitive dissonance). Cognitive dissonance is the mental discomfort (psychological stress) experienced by a person who simultaneously holds two or more contradictory beliefs, ideas or values. As a result, customers are in a different relationship stage compared to prospects, which is also reflected in the differences in the antecedents and consequences for brand trust for both groups. Your brand must therefore consider the differences between customers and prospects and how they represent different perspectives for both groups with regard to social media engagement and corporate reputation.

Corporate reputation management within an SMBC is a balancing act for brands incorporating internal and external potential constructs. These insights are balanced and considered through an ongoing dialogue and sense-making by managers who must try to come to terms with these challenges and to manage corporate reputation effectively on social media communities. One of the main reasons for brands to develop SMBCs is the assumption that they are beneficial for their corporate reputation. Brands are keen to be reputable with consumers and use reputation as a competitive edge and therefore may be keen to develop their SMBC as a mechanism for reputation and innovation. Another additional area that requires further consideration is the legal ramifications that organizations can potentially face when posting content or engaging with consumers. It is crucial that brands consider how to operate within the social media environment and understanding the legal pitfalls and maintaining a professional approach can help to protect their reputation.

When it comes to developing your SMBC brand reputation strategy there are six sub-processes that you can review to help achieve your objectives, which are conceptualized in Figure 13 (below).

FIGURE 13 *SMBC Brand Reputation*

Consumer Fans

Do follower/fan numbers make a difference? A common mistake that brands make is assuming their social media engagement is just a numbers game – i.e. the more followers you have, the more trustworthy you may seem. But the numbers don't always add up and consumers are becoming increasingly savvy to accounts that have suddenly gained 300,000 followers overnight. This is usually achieved with automated tools and bots (autonomous programs on a network(s) which can interact with systems or users) that are set up to create a huge number of fake accounts. This simply won't work for your organization and you can't expect customers to trust your brand on that basis. The SMBC member number alone does not serve to establish trust but must be supplemented with further product and industry information. To increase their reach, some brands incorporate 'liking' into their promotional activities, such as '"like" our page to be entered into a free competition'. The insinuation here is that consumers 'like' the page for the proposed tangible benefit of receiving a prize and not to receive information and product updates from the brand. However, this suggests that 'liking' or 'following' a page represents a weak connection and cannot actively portray the consumer trusting the integrity of the brand with regard to product/service offering.

Products and innovation

The quality and quantity of products available and promoted through an SMBC can also impact reputation. Regarding innovation, brands are able to utilize SMBCs to gauge opinion and develop products on the basis of consumer recommendations potentially utilized in the form of polls, or posts requesting consumer feedback.

Innovative and forward-thinking digital marketing campaigns have the potential to entertain, inspire and educate your target audience and crucially enhance your brand's reputation. The ever-increasing number of social technologies available to companies allows the possibility of creating innovative and memorable campaigns. For example, global athletic brand Adidas are well aware of the impact creative campaigns have on their reputation and are consistently looking at ways to compete with their main rival Nike when engaging with consumers. In April 2018, Adidas used a highly creative approach to digital marketing when they engaged with the runners of the Boston Marathon to create personalized videos showcasing runners wearing their latest running products. The campaign incorporated a combination of professionally produced user-generated content and emerging technologies such as race bibs equipped with high-tech tracker chips. A portal was provided for viewers to feel like they were at the event and to get a sense of the excitement. The campaign also highlighted the individual achievement of the runners by providing running metrics to display their progress during the run. This unique approach was a huge success for Adidas as the personal, emotive and immersive experiences shared were inspirational as well as innovative and resulted in 100,000 video views in the first two days following the race.

Product collaboration

The widespread integration of the Internet by corporations into their strategy and consumers into their daily lives has enhanced the opportunities for collaboration between brands. In online environments, organizations can leverage each other's capabilities as opposed to competing with each other in order to co-exist while still maintaining profitability. Collaboration can take many forms and can involve promoting one another's products or sharing each other's services to increase reach through or improve search ranking, one example being BMW and Louis Vuitton. The two brands may not sound like the most obvious partners, but both are known for producing high-quality products.

The shared values are exactly why working together made so much sense to the decision makers. As part of the collaboration BMW created a sports car model called the BMW i8, while Louis Vuitton designed an exclusive, four-piece set of suitcases and bags to fit perfectly into the car's storage compartment. As Patrick-Louis Vuitton, head of special orders at Louis Vuitton stated

'This collaboration with BMW epitomises our shared values of creativity, technological innovation and style. Our craftsmen have enjoyed the challenge of this very special project, using their ingenuity and attention to detail to create a truly made-to-measure set of luxury luggage. This is a pure expression of the art of travel.'

Responsiveness

A crucial issue for brands when managing corporate reputation through social media is the level of responsiveness. Within seconds of posting a message, millions of consumers are able to 'like', 'retweet', 'check-in' and more around an organization's content. Businesses therefore need to have sufficient plans in place for this level of service.

As a consequence of embracing social media, organizations should avoid the traditional top-down communication models and build open, qualitative and trustworthy dialogues with stakeholders in social media to increase consumer awareness and perception. However, organizations lose their dominance over information flows as they are now exposed to negative word of mouth, which is capable of very quickly affecting reputation adversely. In addition to losing control over information flows, companies could also lose their influence over stakeholder relations and communications between their various stakeholder groups.

When participating in social media companies should instil a proactive communications approach in order to reduce the risk of losing online reputation and have the ability to rectify such situations. The growth of social media in recent years, coupled with the importance of e-WOM for organizations and consumers in social communities, makes the construct of service delivery and competency very interesting for brands. Consumers can perceive effective service delivery through two core constructs: Service information and Consumer Positive/Negative endorsement, conceptualized in Figure 14.

Figure 14 represents the two-way iterative nature of service delivery from e-WOM whereby brand Service Delivery is an interplay of sub-processes including 'Product/Service Information' and 'Consumer Positive/Negative Endorsement'. Social media can establish and raise awareness of the products/services that a brand can offer consumers. By promoting products, brands consider SMBCs suitable platforms to instigate traffic for their website and make more online sales. An SMBC

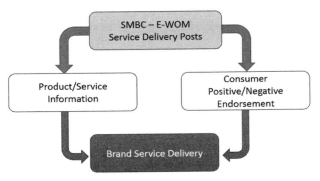

FIGURE 14 *SMBC Brand Service Delivery*

can also give organizations the opportunity to increase the perception of 'competence' by delivering an engaging social media platform and by responding to customer problems efficiently and effectively. So, your service delivery can be defined as a continuous cyclical process for developing and delivering products or services to consumers. By using social media, your brand can implement and promote this process to customers in order to build trust, which is conceptualized in Figure 15 (below).

The Social Media Service Delivery Cycle is made up of four cyclical stages, namely, consumer enquiry, response, delivery and evaluation:

- the first stage – 'Consumer Enquiry' – concerns an analysis of what the customer is requesting;
- the second stage – 'Response' – covers the brand acknowledging the consumer issue and providing a resolution;

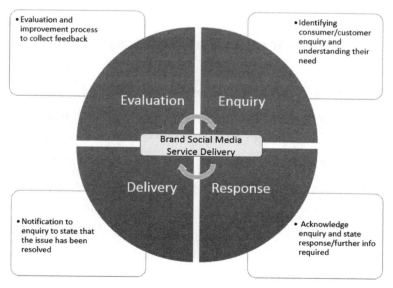

FIGURE 15 *Social Media Service Delivery Cycle*

- third, 'Delivery', acts as an indication from the brand to the consumer (e.g. direct message on Twitter) that the issue has been resolved;
- And finally, 'Evaluation' allows the brand a chance to review the issue to ensure it is not repeated.

In a SMBC context, the role of e-WOM is meaningful as a complementary source of information used by the brand and consumer in order to reduce uncertainty associated with purchasing decisions. Regarding consumer comments, when the comment is positive, it tends to be a result of the customer's satisfaction with the product or service. It could therefore be argued that this emotional state is positively related with the dissemination of e-WOM. However, if e-WOM is negative, it is expected that it will affect the valence of the associations held by consumers towards the brand, thereby influencing trust. In particular, a lack of social media post credibility may cause a simultaneous rejection by consumers, which in turn might provoke a rejection of the social media community.

Personal responses/workplace

Building strong brand trust through social media and utilizing those channels as a means of being more emotionally connected to consumers can be highly beneficial to all businesses. While the messages are not technically 'personal' as they are posted to everyone within the SMBC, they demonstrate appreciation for a consumer's business and well wishes in a non-commercial context. By providing insights into their working day and effectively, their personality, employees are able to connect with consumers. It is important for a brand's employees, who are responsible for social media content, to have flexibility, autonomy and authority to meet the needs of their customers and share personal experiences.

Managing your corporate reputation crisis through social media

In life and in business, hearing the word 'crisis' can be daunting and even quite scary but it is inevitable and at times unavoidable that something will go wrong for your organization. But there is a positive side to all this: in preparing for potential nightmare scenarios you are able to develop new strategies, utilize new technologies and have a focused review of your organization's strong and weak points. Managing a brand crisis is a key part of any company's success and your social media channels provide you with a mechanism to handle such challenges. Due to its speed and accessibility, social media can make or break your reputation but crucially, it can be an invaluable tool to help overcome crisis situations and most importantly, can help your organization prevent them. Even if you manage your business's reputation in a careful and considered way, there is always the possibility that one day you could face a crisis. Other channels such as press releases and email campaigns are both relevant and useful, but they can't 'put out the fires' of a reputation crisis as quick as social media. With its speed in mind, it is crucial that you have a social media crisis communication strategy so that if one day you are faced with a crisis then you have a plan to meet that challenge head-on. Companies can lose control over stakeholder relations and communications between various stakeholder groups so in some instances social media increases the risk of reputational damage. There are three scenarios in which SMBCs could potentially increase the reputation risk that brands are exposed to:

1   While the content in social media is user-generated, social media users can publish true and false facts concerning a company or distribute information that differs from that which companies are willing to share.

2   Social media can enhance expectations (e.g. regarding the ethical behaviour and transparency of companies), which companies might not be able to fulfil.

3   Reputation risk results from the dialogues and behaviour of companies engaged in social media, including reactions to conversations held or the potential manipulation of information (e.g. facts about the company on Wikipedia) and activist influencers in social media (e.g. the bribing of popular bloggers).

Companies must participate in social media in order to observe conversations and correct potentially false information which consumers may be exposed to. If an organization acknowledges a potentially negative issue, then the tone of a discussion can change entirely and may be beneficial in repairing the reputation of a company.

When participating in social media, companies should instil a proactive communications approach to reduce the risk of losing their online reputation and to have the ability to rectify such situations. There are numerous software packages that can monitor consumer conversations and discuss a variety of things connected to your brand, such as sales, employee experience, events or supply chains that you need to be aware of. Using ever-evolving algorithms, these software packages use artificial intelligence to trawl the Internet and can provide easy-to-understand, digestible information, such as sentiment analysis for your brand and how mentions of your brand can develop into problematic or risky situations. In the previous chapter we discussed how vital it is to create and develop an engaged audience by generating and sharing valuable and relevant content through your SMBCs, but it is also vital to track what is being said, listen to the conversations and monitor any conversations taking place. This approach can provide crucial insight into how you are perceived by your audience and can help you shape your message or response accordingly in good times and bad.

So, what does a social media crisis look like? Well, receiving a couple of negative comments on your Facebook page isn't ideal but neither is it exactly a crisis. In reality, many businesses have to handle complaints or unhappy customers every day and we've discussed how they can be converted to build trust through transparency. However, a crisis can start slowly and quickly build momentum and if you start to notice a higher-than-expected volume of posts linked to a specific subject or hashtag mentioning your brand, a crisis could be on the horizon. It's important to stay calm at this point and there are a number of crisis indicators you can identify before any action is taken. First, look at the 'balance of information' being shared and discussed. If the public knows more than your communications team or more than you have shared publicly, this is a definite cause for concern. Also, consider any potential 'behaviour change' in your comments, i.e. are you suddenly facing criticism not connected to regular day-to-day activity? The spread or 'reach of criticism' can also be a concern – are your mentions becoming so frequent that they are trending or are you being criticized by an individual with a huge following? Finally, consider the 'complexity of response': if the situation absolutely requires the attention of the CEO or the board of directors due to its complicated nature then you are most definitely at crisis point.

The 'Crisis Source' – i.e. how the crisis starts – can potentially originate from a number of channels. It may start if a company makes a mistake when posting through their SMBC or from an individual who is attacking your brand on their personal account. A crisis source can literally come from anywhere or anyone and can spread really quickly, but while the speed of social media can work against you in this situation, with the right plan in place you can reverse the situation and make it work for you. The key here is to take control of the crisis as soon as possible and confront the situation with a clear position statement, which includes acknowledgement (awareness there is an issue), accountability (highlighting responsibility for the issue, internal or external) and action (what are you going to do to resolve the issue?). This approach can also be applied when the crisis source is technically outside of your control, such as a natural disaster. To maintain trust in your brand you need to clarify what exactly has happened and what will happen to alleviate your audience's concerns. There are a number of steps you can take to plan and co-ordinate your response (below).

How to monitor the situation

Due to the sheer volume of messages in which you may be mentioned or tagged, across multiple social media channels, it might be beneficial to use social media monitoring software that helps you identify factors such as hashtags created as a result of the crisis, the key influencers who are forthright in discussions around the crisis, as well as the social or communications channels where the crisis needs to be first addressed. If resource is an issue and funds are not available for specialized software, there are free options available via commercial companies as well as the platforms themselves, such as Twitter. However, the depth and analysis they provide can be limited, so determining employee responsibility for monitoring becomes all-important.

Just as a celebrity can make an error of judgement when engaging on social media that leads to widespread criticism and embarrassment, so too can organizations. Employees who run the social media accounts for major brands can be responsible for some massive social media mistakes when posting online. At some point in our lives, we've all posted or shared something we regretted, but imagine sharing something that was in poor taste, or not factually accurate, and which on the face of it then reflects the thoughts and opinions of a company with thousands of employees. One such incident happened earlier in 2018 when Snapchat posted an advert that appeared to make light of singer Rihanna's 2009 domestic abuse incident with then boyfriend, fellow singer Chris Brown. The ad that Snapchat posted was for a new app called 'Would You Rather', which was based on a popular party game where players have to try to choose the most preferential between two unpleasant scenarios. The ad was in particularly poor taste as it asked users, 'Would you rather slap Rihanna or punch Chris Brown?'. Despite most likely being a misguided attempt at humour, it was completely inappropriate.

This understandably caused uproar among fans and led to Snapchat issuing an apology, stating the ad had been mistakenly approved to go live but was removed as soon as other company officials became aware of its content. Rihanna dismissed the apology and posted an emotional response via Instagram condemning the app for ridiculing domestic abuse victims everywhere. As you can imagine, this had a huge negative impact on Snapchat's reputation.

Preparing your crisis response

Before you start, it's important to emphasize that not all crises are the same so the plan you prepare must be as flexible and considered as possible to be achievable with the resources you have at your disposal. To begin with, it's a good idea to sit down with your team and discuss potential crisis scenarios and determine who would be involved in preparing and managing your response so consider who is responsible for:

- assessment of crisis/situation analysis;
- the nature of the responses (spokesperson or a response team) and characteristics of them (in particular, tone and voice), as well as your social media and customer-facing teams' involvement;
- monitoring the crisis and providing updates.

This could involve forming a crisis social media sub-group or team that involves representatives from different departments. The team could take the lead for scenario planning, software analysis and reviewing your crisis governance principles. These principles can contain guidelines that your organization follows when dealing with crisis situations through social media. They can also act as guidelines for employees who use their own social media accounts to promote brand activity or in some instances criticize the company. The principles should also state the style, tone and voice for any responses.

Handling a crisis

'The ultimate measure of a man is not where he stands in moments of comfort and convenience, but where he stands at times of challenge and controversy.'

Not to take anything away from this wonderfully inspirational quote from Martin Luther King Jr, but the same can be applied to brands in crisis. Put simply, you can tell a lot about someone by how they handle and deal with a crisis and the same goes for a business. A social media crisis can arise for a number of reasons, such as a poorly judged marketing campaign or an accidental Instagram post. These situations can escalate quickly, so it's vital that your organization has a plan of action covering how to act and respond, publicly and internally. So let's now look at how some brands coped with social media crises and what strategies did and didn't work for them.

A lot of the time, a crisis can happen out of nowhere. This was just the case for fast food chain Taco Bell, who were sued in 2011 for allegedly using just 35 per cent beef in their meat products, with the claim stating the remaining 65 per cent contained water, wheat, oats, maltodextrin and other 'fake' ingredients. The accusation was made by an individual, but the story spread quickly on social media. There was even further coverage through the mainstream media but Taco Bell refused to panic and instead considered how to go about promoting their response. The claim was vehemently denied by the brand but in response to the accusation they launched an entire marketing campaign based around it, creating videos of President Greg Creed discussing the ingredients of their products and sharing them through their social media channels. The company also followed up with print ads educating their customers with the accurate ingredients list for their products and joked, 'Thank you for not suing us.'

Although this example might be considered more of a brand crisis than a social media one, it still shows how SMBCs can be utilized to change consumer perceptions quickly. Taco Bell controlled the situation by focusing their response on marketing via their Facebook and Twitter channels, so the organization successfully reached and engaged customers, which resulted in a wave of supportive comments in support of the brand's campaign. This example shows that effective social media crisis management is not just about how to respond in the short term, but finding ways to repair your reputation and look to enhance it long after the initial incident has happened. The key takeaway from this example is that more and more consumers are using social media for current information and updates, so these channels are a great platform to very quickly halt any rumours or controversy. No matter if the crisis is large or small, an open and honest response will always be the most effective course of action.

Isaac Newton's laws of motion are three physical laws that together laid the foundation for classical mechanics. The laws describe the relationship between a body and the forces acting upon it and its motion in response to those forces. Newton's third law essentially states that for every action, there is an equal and opposite reaction. This law could also be applied in a way to how you respond to a crisis: if the crisis is big, respond in equal measure. Unfortunately, this was not the approach that British Airways (BA) used when handling their own crisis.

Brands often post updates on their social channels to apologize for poor service or provide real time updates if there are any expected delays. It's a great way to keep your customers up to date but as you can appreciate it can often lead to heavy criticism with a raft of complaints left as comments underneath the post. This was the approach adopted by British Airways in 2017 when their IT systems crashed, an incident that grounded thousands of passengers at London's Heathrow and Gatwick airports. Again, BA were open and honest and admitted their failure by posting a video of Chief Executive Alex Cruz apologizing on Twitter but sometimes sorry isn't enough and instead of bringing the issue to a close, the video caused further outrage among passengers, who criticized the CEO for the lack of information that BA had provided. In this instance a video saying sorry was an inappropriate response for the magnitude of the crisis; one tweet with an apology seemed superficial and disingenuous and wasn't enough to make up for the stress and anxiety that their customers had gone through due to BA's technical failure. As a result, BA received considerable criticism, not just in social media environments but via mainstream media coverage as well.

With any social crisis it's important to reflect on your activity and assess if it could have been handled better. Though annoying for customers on the whole, they will understand that sometimes issues can occur and so keeping them informed as much as possible is crucial. But BA's poorly timed and inadequate response only fuelled customers' anger. Instead of using their social media channels to respond to queries and provide updates, they just used them to say sorry after the error had happened. This isn't the best way to use your social media channels for customer service at any time, let alone in the midst of a full-blown crisis. The main lesson here is to respond with information that customers will want to hear, even if the nature of the update isn't always favourable.

Sometimes promotional campaigns gain attention for the wrong reasons, which is what happened to sleepwear company Lunya in 2018. To capitalize on the popularity of the TV show, *The Handmaid's Tale*, the company wanted to build brand awareness for their products and named the latest red product in its range, 'Offred', which was a play on words inspired by the show's main protagonist. This was a risky approach as the TV show covers serious themes based on the oppression and slavery of women. Despite using taglines on their social media channels such as 'join the resistance', referring to the patriarchal society represented on the show, the strategy and product was completely inappropriate due to the sensitivities around such emotive topics. In this instance, Lunya faced negative mainstream media coverage and significant criticism on social media for their insensitive approach. Here, the key takeaway is to try and resist the 'piggyback' approach to your brand and social media strategy unless the social phenomena you align yourself with is linked to your brand values. Being controversial and highlighting difficult emotive topics can make your brand stand out among your competitors and empower your campaign. Nevertheless, unless your product/service offering and brand values are aligned with the 'popular' theme, this should be avoided.

To be successful in business it has become vital for nearly all employees within an organization to learn and develop skills which are essential for business relationship-building and online marketing. Consequently, more and more often employees are now having to act as social media advocates for their organization. As a result, individual employees are likely to be seen as social media ambassadors, with their online activities reflecting on the brand, whether or not they represent it officially online. However, in order for your brand to manage the risk of potential negative publicity arising from comments that have been posted online, or poor behaviour from your employees, all employees should be trained in the appropriate and sensible use of social media and in the types of skills needed to demonstrate this.

To instigate, develop and maintain a strong and positive digital presence and brand personality, your company should look to create specific social media management roles. Many organizations recognized the benefits of having specific social media roles a long time ago or may even outsource to social media PR agencies. However, having in-house specialist social media officers for at least the non-technical aspects of the work is important since these employees will act as official representatives for your company. For this to be an effective tactic, the social media officers must be given the freedom to respond in an authoritative and consistent way to comments and feedback, as well as giving them the opportunity to create and post content reflecting the brand's values and showcasing the organization's activity.

Sales

Sales analysis for SMBCs generally relates back to marketing analytics, which historically, have tended to be more about product than customer, i.e. incremental units sold or, less helpfully, incremental conversations. Within social media it's really difficult to find examples of organizations that have seamlessly replicated the process that initially got the consumer to them in the first place. To that extent analytics from specific promotional activity are often used to measure relationships.

The promotional approach (i.e. discounts/sales offers) to social media has staying power and promotional activities are also the foundation for many social media posts – reflected, for example, on Facebook, Twitter and other popular sites whose facilities are used, among other things, for posting promotions. In this regard, consumer value is founded on providing useful information to those who choose to interact, focusing not so much on return on investment (ROI) as return on attention. Your brand should focus on getting the attention of consumers first, with engaging content that creates trust, before beginning to analyse the tangible benefits associated with SMBCs. When it comes to selling specialized services that brands can provide, the value of social media monitoring can be a difficult concept for brands to understand and utilize. Nevertheless, due to the amount of consumers on social media, it will always be an attractive environment for brands and sales can be viewed as a key indicator of ROI.

Customer service

In order to develop and sustain trust through engagement, some brands include customer service as part of their SMBC strategy. In particular, brands need to pay attention to consumer service issues to reassure prospects through a clear representation of problem resolution, as well as assuring existing customers that any potential issue will be resolved quickly. The associated considerations are represented in Figure 16 (below).

FIGURE 16 *SMBC Customer Service Considerations*

Customer service through an SMBC – in particular, as a trust mechanism – is a key aspect of successful brand/consumer engagement. Establishing a social media customer service process is imperative for facilitating consumer transactions and for indicating trustworthy e-business. Having a system in place for customer service empowers staff to have access to social media and to be able to provide the service through social media. This links the concept of customer service as an engagement mechanism to Connection, Value, Satisfaction and Loyalty themes in terms of efficiency, speed of service and as a reassuring factor to consumers. If brands are monitoring customer value with each post and more customer service enquiries are handled through social media, brands may see more repeat purchases not only from providing the customer service, but also from engaging content.

There are drawbacks to handling all enquiries through an SMBC, however. Some consumers feel that they are able to publicly attack brands via these channels in order to receive the desired outcome. To prepare for these scenarios, it is imperative that brands have procedures in place to handle such enquiries, which include efficiency and speed of response. Say, for example, a brand receives a customer complaint or something similar and then someone makes a negative comment on it; if not replied to or reacted to quick enough it can then lead to mistrust rather than developing the trust itself. That's a major concern for any organization.

Evaluation

Measuring the business value from IT has traditionally been problematic and this extends to social media. While the impact of traditional online activity can be measured using defined quantitative metrics, social media generates a huge amount of qualitative data, which traditional metrics alone do not address or quantify in monetary terms. The key to unlocking the value of an SMBC relies on consumer conversation, which requires the ability to track the tone, perception and nuances of comments, making it extremely difficult for brands to measure and quantify.

Measuring engagement

Measuring your customer engagement is intrinsically connected to the influence or strength of your SMBC. Consequently, there are different metrics you can utilize to review the effectiveness and impact of your engagement activity. As a result, there are a number of metrics you can keep an eye on to see how effective your SMBC engagement is by your website commercial transactions and CRM updates, which include:

- **Guest checkout rates** – The lower the number of guest checkouts you have, the more 'new customers' are creating an account on your website and engaging with your brand;
- **Purchase frequency** – A higher purchase frequency means customers are returning and engaging with your website more often;
- **Average order value** – An increase in average order value indicates that customers are forming emotional connections with your brand and are choosing to stay loyal to your organization's offering;
- **Customer lifetime value** – The emotional connections customers develop with your community, which will translate into a higher financial commitment over time;
- **Churn and retention rates** – The lower your customer churn rate, the more committed customers are to staying engaged with your brand community.

If you include these customer engagement metrics as part of your daily key performance indicators (KPIs), they will form an important piece of your brand's daily analytics. These metrics will then help inform the rest of your data analysis and provide you with the insight you need to continue to update and refine your customers' SMBC experience.

A lack of definitive quantitative measures, such as return on investment (ROI) of time and money, might be considered a hindrance to the continued use of social media by brands who require evidence of value in both the short and longer term. Nevertheless, applying metrics enables the capturing of some levels of information and the measurements are often given as evidence of success within organizations. However, more qualitative measures are required to fully capture the extent of value that can be derived from social media use. There are of course a number of platforms available (e.g. Google Analytics, Hootsuite) to assist in this type of analysis and we'll discuss some research methods later in Chapter 5. However, the importance of recognizing what to do with the analysis is of paramount importance for brands, in particular attributing objectives to specific channels and utilizing the statistics.

Measurement software provides metrics for brand awareness, brand competitiveness and brand likeability. The 'net promoter score' is also an indicator of customers' attitudes derived from measuring the customer's likelihood to recommend the organization or products to other consumers. These metrics provide a more qualitative view of consumers but they can still potentially reinforce volume-oriented thinking and thus may be inadequate as proxies for quantitative insights. Engaging staff in this way can also improve relationships with consumers and develop trust by identifying current consumer trends. Training staff on the importance of customer-focused and integrated activities also has the added benefit of improving trust by improving enquiry response times, which carries the bonus of enhancing service satisfaction levels, which in turn encourages customer retention and positive e-WOM among consumers.

The importance of having a system of approach to analysing the quality of social media feedback is well known to brands, however organizations need to be mindful that one piece of software may not cover all the analytics required to achieve their corporate objectives. Brands have to have KPIs and will naturally look at how many times a piece of content was re-Tweeted, shared, or commented on. But it is crucial that any statistical analysis must align with additional marketing activity (the rest of your marketing activities, the rest of your PR activities and the rest of your customer service relationships).

Financial gains can be measured in monetary value. Non-financial gains from SMBCs may be equally beneficial for brands, resulting in a range of benefits such as increased awareness and trust. Despite reported successes for numerous organizations, the ongoing measurement debate highlighted in this chapter shows there is a need for brands to adopt a transparent, consistent, yet flexible measurement framework.

Summary

Return on investment (ROI) for social media can be analysed in two forms for brands, financial and non-financial. As previously highlighted, social media can aid the generation of revenue for organizations as communities can be used as promotional platforms for products or services. In respect of the potential non-financial ROI, key areas include increased engagement and developing brand reputation. SMBCs can be extremely useful to brands as they are capable of providing platforms that contribute to the interactions and transactions between consumers and businesses.

As social media is an ever-changing business environment, due to new technological innovations, a flexible model is required to meet the measurement needs of brands. One of the main criticisms of existing models is that they appear to be overcomplicated, presenting complicated management and evaluation processes, which may be off-putting for organizations. As a result, any SMBC should be adaptable due to the changing needs of consumers and flexible strategic models are required which are straightforward to implement for brands incorporating measurement and evaluation activity. By using such a model, brands would be encouraged to adopt a more strategic focus when planning, implementing and measuring SMBC activity. A conceptual framework that provides direction for brands to evaluate ROI on a SMBC is presented below in Figure 17.

The model is fairly simplistic and can be applied to organizations of all sizes while being flexible enough to be adapted to meet the needs of an organization. The framework consists of the brand identifying their corporate objectives and then evaluating available resource, followed by four themes: target audience, reputation, sales, customer services. The next theme, evaluation, considers both short-term and long-term value of SMBC engagement when all five themes are combined as part of a sequential framework to provide brand SMBC corporate value. The planning stage should involve setting goals, defining objectives and outlining suitable metrics for measuring the impact of social media.

Previous models that analyse social media ROI argue that clearly defined objectives and evaluation metrics must be agreed upon prior

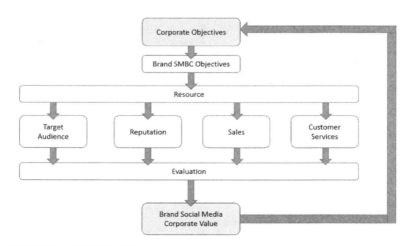

FIGURE 17 *ROI SMBC*

to an organization's entry into the social media arena and that they should influence any decision on which SMBCs and analytical tools an organization should use to measure and deliver results. Consequently, brands must know what they hope to achieve through their SMBCs before they enter into the social media environment. Therefore, the ever-changing and complicated nature of social media necessitates that brands plan their SMBCs strategy with caution. Before creating an SMBC, organizations need to be aware of what consumers are interested in as this can help drive appropriate engagement goals and may inform the decision of which social media platform to utilize. The creation and development of any SMBC requires a long-term investment and as social media is all about 'people' and 'relationships', brands need to invest time in developing effective relationships with customers in order to ensure positive outcomes. When measuring ROI, the focus on financial returns must not be lost for brands, although the benefits associated with intangible conversation and participation need considerable attention as they can lead to future returns.

Previous research highlights 'Credibility' or 'Source expertise' as a significant factor in determining the effectiveness of persuasive communication on social media and trust generation by listening to what consumers have to say. With two core constructs, brand expertise and consumer expertise, supported by two sub-constructs, products and service, conceptualized in Figure 18 (below).

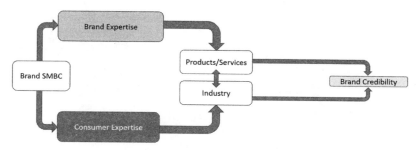

FIGURE 18 *SMBC Credibility*

Figure 18 highlights the credibility constructs which could stem from the risk a consumer may experience before engaging with and subsequently purchasing from a brand and using their SMBC to obtain purchase assurance. Credibility can be promoted via your SMBC by the joint promotion of expertise from the brand and the consumer. The organization's and consumer's expertise can be emphasized with posts or blogs which provide knowledge on product use or industry tips. This method is also connected with brands actively encouraging consumers to share their expertise or tips with fellow community members or using influencers. This activity essentially makes the SMBC a knowledge and information hub which passionate consumers are motivated to visit on a regular basis and prospects are convinced is an informed and trustworthy organization.

Security

Consumer security should also be preserved when exploring trust to improve the SMBC experiences of consumers. Online consumer security is comprised of five sub-constructs which develop trust, which are represented in Figure 19.

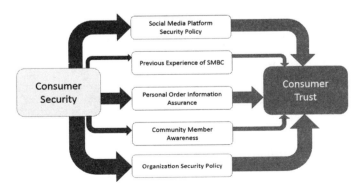

FIGURE 19 *Consumer SMBC Security*

A challenge for brands is how to build trusting relationships among prospects and customers and provide trustworthy content to them. Organizations need to provide transparent data privacy policies to build trust and brand loyalty for all consumers. For organizations that utilize social media communities as a valuable source of consumer insight, it is important that they manage actual and perceived efforts to maintain privileged and confidential consumer privacy information. Social media sites can cause concerns for consumers as they may not be aware of all the brand's policies and they may feel that social networking sites actively engage in sharing some of their members' information to external organizations (e.g. Cambridge Analytica). Organizations can also potentially use information that community members post – for instance, photos to emphasize credibility and essentially create consumer trust for the organization.

Brand responsibilities

We live in an age where we increasingly outsource our trust to technology and specific algorithms, such as searching Facebook for news, booking a cab via Uber and asking Alexa what the weather is like outside. From a commercial perspective, this consumer digital trust means there are new and different challenges for brands in determining how they engage with their customers.

The relationship between brand and consumer, and the transparency which the relationship is based on, risks being disrupted by the growing influence of bots. With the rise of automation, robotics and Artificial Intelligence (AI), bots are able to refine the choices presented and even make choices on behalf of consumers. There is also an argument that the intervention of bots will mean that matters of ethics, which are individual non-binary decisions, will be forgotten. This effectively places even more responsibility on the brand to uphold their ethics. Bots may ignore ethics in the moment of choice, but ultimately, any brand that refuses to meet the requirement for transparent ethics will inevitably risk consumer uproar.

Recent developments are having an impact on the trust we place in digital platforms, particularly how we perceive them and how they operate. Examples such as the 2016 presidential election in the US and the constant uncertainty over 'fake news' accusations, as well as the rescinding of Uber's licence in London have encouraged different trust expectations for the role and responsibilities of companies like Facebook and Uber. Historically, social media companies have positioned themselves as neutral pathways that connect people with each other or products and services. Scandals such as Cambridge Analytica have led to organizations such as Facebook changing their accountability positioning from 'reactive – within reason, to do all they can when things go wrong', to being 'proactive and accepting responsibility for the risks of bad things happening'.

But where does the responsibility lie?

When it comes to trust and digital communications, it really comes down to asking yourself a question, who do you place your trust with? With the platform, e.g. Twitter, or with the brand that has a community on the platform, e.g. Nike Facebook Group? It is this conflict that is causing a decline in trust and is having a significant impact on brands' digital communications.

Due to recent high-profile scandals for social media companies, trust in how a brand is perceived on these digital platforms has never been more important. Indeed, a trust barometer study conducted by Edelman (2018) found that 70 per cent of digitally connected people around the world believe that brands need to pressure social media sites to do more to counter fake news and false information proliferating on their sites and that 71 per cent expect brands to pressure social media platforms to protect personal data. The study collected responses from 1,000 consumers online from nine markets around the world between 16 and 30 April 2018. The findings were certainly revealing when it comes to consumers' expectations of brands on social media, with almost 50 per cent of respondents considering it to be the brand's fault if its advertising appeared alongside hate speech or other inappropriate content online.

'Consumers are looking at the brands just as much as – if not more than – the actual platforms,' Kevin King, global chair of Edelman Digital, said in an interview in 2018. 'You can't just point to Facebook or Google or Twitter. The consumer is not making a huge distinction between the brand and the platform.'

According to the Edelman research findings, 60 per cent of respondents stated that social media is the most effective place for brands to deliver customer service and 51 per cent said social media was one of the best platforms to introduce new products to consumers. However, the research highlighted a widespread decline in trust in social media platforms. In the United States in particular, trust in social media had dropped 11 points year-over-year to 30 per cent. Nevertheless, some of the accountability is understandably perceived to be with the actual social media platform. The study also found that 40 per cent of digitally connected consumers thought social media was doing a good job of controlling the spread of false information and controlling hate speech or other forms of online harassment, with 60 per cent of respondents claiming they don't trust social media companies to behave ethically with personal data. Furthermore, 70 per cent of respondents said fake news, clickbait, cyberbullying and hate speech all contributed to lowering their trust in social media.

Indeed, there are now a number of global brands threatening to pull money from big advertisers if they do not resolve illegal content issues on their websites. These organizations simply don't want to be associated with fake news and no wonder they aren't happy with how this reflects on their brand.

For example, Unilever has asked that Facebook and other social media websites take on the responsibility of transparency and start to combat fake news and terrorist content. Chief Marketing Officer for Unilever, Keith Weed, made an interesting speech surrounding the issues, stating, 'It is critical that our brands remain not only in a safe environment, but a suitable one. Fake news, racism, sexism, terrorists spreading messages of hate, toxic content directed at children... it is in the digital media industry's interest to listen and act on this. Before viewers stop viewing, advertisers stop advertising and publishers stop publishing.'

Nevertheless, Facebook are fighting back in the war on fake news, developing forensic methods to identify what content is up to date and accurate. Such methods were recently highlighted by Facebook Product Manager Antonia Woodford, in a 2018 Facebook Newsroom blog, who sought to reaffirm Facebook's commitment to eradicating fake news by stating, 'Every day, Facebook fights the spread of false news through a combination of technology and assessments from independent third-party fact-checkers. With every false story that surfaces, we learn a bit more about how misinformation takes shape online and, hopefully, how we can detect it earlier.' This mission was highlighted in recent case studies which Facebook released to show to their users that they are actively looking to increase trust in the platform's content. For instance, in the summer of 2018, a video featuring CCTV footage was re-shared by multiple accounts across several social networks. In the video, a man wearing a white robe and a shemagh (head scarf) spat in the face of a blonde woman in what appeared to be a hospital reception area. The accompanying caption read, 'Man from Saudi spits in the face of the poor receptionist at a hospital in London then attacks other staff'. Indeed, while the video was in fact real, the incident actually occurred in a veterinary hospital in Kuwait in 2017 and was being recirculated with a falsified caption. According to Facebook, one of the main types of video- and photo-based misinformation involves old images or videos which are paired with captions or commentary that misrepresents their actual context. These posts are often used to incite xenophobic sentiments and are often targeted at migrants and refugees, as the International Fact-Checking Network, the association certifying the third-party fact-checkers that partners with Facebook, has claimed (Facebook Newsroom, 2018). Facebook are now using two primary ways to determine if stories are likely to be false. They either use machine learning to detect potentially false stories on Facebook, or they are identified by their third-party fact-checkers themselves. In this case, they found the video to be out of context. Once a potentially false story has been identified, regardless of how it was found, their fact-checkers review the claims, rate their accuracy and provide an explanation as to how they arrived at their rating. They investigated this video and its caption and submitted a 'false' rating and explainer article, which subsequently led Facebook to reduce its distribution on their news feed.

One further example involved the surprisingly named website World Facts FTW, who claimed NASA were looking to compensate volunteers up to $100,000 to participate in 60-day 'bed-rest studies'. Such a sensational amount of money for very little hard work naturally garnered attention, with the post racking up millions of views on Facebook. This too-good-to-be-true story warranted further investigation and a further Facebook partner, US-based fact-checker Politifact, investigated the story. While they found that NASA has indeed paid people to stay in bed for long periods of time, the headline of this particular story was incredibly misleading. The photos in the World Facts FTW article came from a 2015 *Vice* article about a NASA medical research study for which the author stayed in bed for 70 days but was only paid $18,000, not $100,000 (Politifact utilized a reverse image search to find the *Vice* article.) Politifact was unable to get verification for the $100,000 claim from either NASA or World Facts FTW, so they then rated the article's central claim as false.

Facebook are improving their content verification and they are getting better at detecting and removing fake news, even as perpetrators' tactics continue to evolve, but as with the NASA example, content can take a long time to verify and by the time all the checks have been completed, the damage may have been done and many will have been influenced under false pretences. However, Facebook are adamant that they will continue to develop new technology to catch these kinds of stories in the future before they go viral.

Summary

Social media platforms allow brands the opportunity to engage with consumers using interactive content to create brand trust and encourage community members to become active, loyal and advocating customers. The challenge for brands is determining which strategies their organization should adopt in order to engage consumers to build brand trust in social media. Consumer engagement that builds brand trust can be reviewed by analysing a consumer's motivation to become engaged and develop a relationship with an organization. The main motivations a consumer may have for engaging include the financial, cognitive and social benefits received through SMBC interaction. Organizations can also benefit from such interaction and from a strategic perspective it is vital for brands to understand how they can promote the engagement that they have with consumers and enhance trust for the brand. Engagement strategies within social media platforms should always be connected with the various stages that a consumer goes through when interacting with a brand but also the consumer/brand trust stage that they are at. The strategies at each stage of social media engagement can then influence the level of trust associated with the brand. Thus, it is crucial for your brand to understand the role and importance of social networks for consumers and how the content will support the existing marketing mix within the organization.

This section set out to guide brands on how to structure and create campaigns that foster consumer engagement for prospects and customers. Social media enables consumers to participate in value adding by connecting and interacting not only with brands, but also with other customers as well as prospects. A key challenge for organizations is to connect with current as well as potential customers and encourage their opinion and involvement in developing products and services that meet consumer needs. By involving consumers in the value creation process, the likelihood of satisfaction increases and further progression through the social media engagement framework occurs. In satisfying consumers, brands can develop strong emotional connections or develop lasting relationships with them. Continuous interaction between organizations and consumers utilizing different social media platforms can also enhance customer retention by creating affective and/or calculative commitment. Customers with strong emotional bonds can potentially become advocates for brands when interacting with other customers and prospects and play an integral part in the value-adding process as co-creators of value. As the connection becomes more relational and the emotional bonds stronger, brands can in turn become customer advocates who try to do what's best for their customers in order to sustain consumer trust in their brand.

A successful brand engagement strategy which is looking to develop meaningful relationships with a target audience will typically see messages in social media marketing co-ordinated with messages in other channels. Disney, as you would expect, has a strong presence on social media and at the time of writing has six Twitter accounts, 13 Facebook pages, five Instagram accounts and six YouTube accounts in the UK alone. As Anna Hill, Disney's CMO for the UK and Ireland, describes it: 'All elements of our campaigns work together, we know people transition from one medium to another at different points of the day and even at the same time. We want to ensure that we are delivering a consistent message but using the different media to benefit from their key points of strength' (*Marketing Week*, 2018). Utilizing data from such vast different sources is a significant challenge for brands but having effective data management platforms in place allows brands like Disney to understand similar behaviours across different brand engagements and act on those insights. For instance, if a user engages with content around a particular film then it is able to harness that information to provide them with similar content first, on a range of channels such as email and social media.

There are many different interpretations of integrated marketing and what it actually means for your organization, but true integration essentially means mapping your strategy to align with your customer's reality. Consider your target audience's daily routine and how your messages can engage with them at their daily touchpoints. The attention span of your audience is relatively short so you need to ensure that your marketing messages are aligned across all of those touchpoints, which can be experiential or through their mobile device. The most effective integrated marketing campaigns engage with customers by taking a brand's message and customizing it for each part of the customer journey.

Let's look at how this can be achieved by your brand. A great example is incorporating user-generated content (UGC) into each aspect of your digital marketing campaign. Again, using the example of GoPro (digital marketing institute, 2017), the brand has used the theme of 'Be a HERO' to connect with its target audience in a powerful way. Using brand-related sponsorships and endorsements, outdoor ads, SEO, Web and targeted social media, GoPro integrates all of their marketing activity with engaging UGC. Once a brand has decided to create an SMBC it has to define, implement and follow up specific activities on the selected social media to consistently look to engage with consumers in order to develop initial and continual trust.

5

Conducting Social Media Research

Researching consumer wants and needs and consistently meeting their expectations is crucial for all brands. Many organizations use research or analytics software to uncover trends in consumer behaviour, allowing it to adjust its offerings and tailor digital promotions to customers. However, there is also the necessity for brands to conduct further in-depth research to keep up to date with customer opinions.

From a data analysis perspective, the Internet provides many opportunities for gathering observational data on a large scale and for using data to construct, test and adapt models of how consumers behave in a digital environment. Utilizing the methods available to conduct research gives you or your organization the opportunity to thrive in a fast-moving, competitive and constantly changing environment. Indeed, you could even consider the Internet and social media in general to be a huge focus group, with uninhibited consumers offering up their thoughts for free. As a result, customer-generated (or expert-generated) information about a specific brand could be considered as valuable a source of research for your brand as more formal market and media research. In the fast-changing and turbulent e-commerce markets of today, it is especially important to conduct brand research on a regular basis as consumer behaviour and crucially trust measures can change much faster than any formal market research programme.

In order to carry out effective research it's important to have an understanding of research approaches, so when analysing your social media brand community (SMBC) activity you can consider the philosophical and psychological approach to research and how best to utilize findings to help shape your strategy. To begin with, we'll focus on the philosophical aspects of research.

Philosophical approach to social media research

The most important thing to highlight from the beginning is that there is no right or wrong method for research. Whether you choose to use surveys, interviews, focus groups or digital analytics they can all be relevant and useful. The most important factor for any brand conducting research is deciding which approach works best for them to achieve their objectives. The 'methodology' of any research adopted is founded on two philosophical perspectives, 'Ontology' and 'Epistemology', which will help you comprehend the appropriateness of any approach adopted.

Ontology and epistemology concern a 'theoretical perspective' which basically provides a way of looking at the world and making sense of what is happening around us. Ontology identifies the assumptions made about the nature of reality and refers to 'the study of being'. Closely connected with ontology and its consideration of what constitutes reality, epistemology considers views about the most suitable ways of enquiring into the nature of the world and the sources and limitations of knowledge. Epistemology primarily deals with the assumptions made by the researcher as to what is possible, the authenticity of knowledge and how that knowledge can be collected with regard to method, validity and scope. This might sound very complicated and may not always be a consideration for any research you or your organization carries out but essentially ontology and epistemology help provide clarity for your research approach. The perspectives are summed up perfectly by leading marketing academic Dr Catherine Ashworth, who said in her 2008 PhD thesis, 'Organizational development, continuity and success in UK SME fashion e-retailing: A critical case approach': 'Ontology and epistemology form the philosophical perspective which informs methodology by contextualizing and grounding the research process in order to utilize an appropriate strategy and to resolve research questions which assists in determining credibility in social research.'

When carrying out social media research there are two contrasting ontological and epistemological perspectives that dominate the discussion regarding the most effective approach. Namely, positivism and social constructionism. Positivism asserts that all authentic knowledge involves verification and all authentic knowledge assumes the only valid knowledge is scientific. Positivism stresses an objective reality independent of humankind can be identified using a deductive approach, adopting scientific measurements to formulate and test hypotheses which establish an assumed objective truth. Alternatively, social constructionism questions the existence of an objective reality since ontologically, it does not assume any pre-existing reality and consequently emphasizes 'the active involvement of people in reality construction' and requires a more iterative approach to analysis.

So, if we break these two perspectives down, positivism is a philosophy which only accepts things that can be seen or proven and is often the approach for laboratory research in natural sciences whereas social constructionism is a theory of knowledge in sociology and communication theory that examines the development of jointly constructed understandings of the world which form the basis for shared assumptions about reality. The theory centres on the notion that meanings are developed in co-ordination with others rather than separately within each individual.

These contrasting perspectives are highlighted in Table 3 (below) which describes particular methods and their research focus. Take a look

TABLE 3 *Research Philosophical Considerations*

Research consideration	Positivist Assumptions	Social Constructionism Assumptions
Ontology and Epistemology	Objective reality exists and can be discovered Possible to obtain objective knowledge of reality through accumulation of data Governed by hypotheses and stated theories and is purportedly value free	Reality is socially constructed (i.e. social phenomena and categories are socially constructed and 'given meaning' by people) Reality understood through 'perceived' knowledge and is value-laden Seeks to understand specific context
Research Focus	Research focuses on generalization (or 'facts') Seeks causality and fundamental laws (i.e. clear distinction between facts & value judgements) Formulate and test hypotheses Units of analysis reduced to simple terms Generalization through statistical probability	Focus on meanings (and perceptions) Seeks to understand what is happening in context to increase general understanding Gather rich data from which ideas are conceptualized Includes complexity of whole situations Generalization through theoretical abstraction (and saturation)
Appropriate Methods	Requires objective or scientific methods – i.e. phenomena require a form of measurement Large sample, random selection, survey approach	Should incorporate stakeholder perspectives Small sample investigation, cases chosen for specific reasons (i.e. theoretical purposive sampling)

Source: Ashworth (2008: 110)

at some of the examples and consider which approach you feel would be suitable for your social media research.

Remember, there's no right or wrong approach to research so be mindful that positivism states an objective reality independent of humankind can be discovered via a deductive approach using scientific measurements to formulate and test hypotheses in order to establish an assumed objective truth. This can potentially be achieved in business research by adopting a survey approach that lends itself to statistical analysis, which could include experimental survey design, allowing data to be treated independently and, assuming a sizeable sample, generalized to a wider population. Positivist research aims to maintain an independent, objective stance, whereby the researcher is distinct, detached and emotionally neutral from the research object. But if you are researching your own business or company that you work for, how objective can you truly be when conducting research?

Alternatively, social constructionism challenges the existence of an objective reality as ontologically it does not assume any pre-existing reality and consequently emphasizes the active involvement of people in reality construction, requiring a more iterative approach to investigation analysis.

Business social construction research can potentially explore the meanings consumers place on events or experiences to enable a contextual understanding to be gained and interpreted. This can then lead to theory building or theory generation, which can help formulate your social media strategy. So again, consider what it is you are trying to achieve when beginning to plan your research and which approach is relevant for your business. This is a really difficult task so to help with your decision we can look at the type of data (qualitative or quantitative) you wish to collect and how you would analyse it.

Which approach is the most suitable, qualitative or quantitative?

Quantitative research is the systematic empirical investigation of observable phenomena via statistical, mathematical or computational techniques. In the social sciences, the term relates to empirical methods, originating in both philosophical positivism and the history of statistics, which directly contrast with qualitative research methods. Whereas qualitative analysis is the analysis of data (e.g. data from interview transcripts) that is dependent on the researcher's analytic and interrogative skills and personal knowledge of the social context where the data is collected, quantitative analysis involves statistics largely independent of the researcher. In qualitative analysis, rather than explaining or predicting, sense-making must be emphasized in order to understand the experience. Alternatively, qualitative research is centred on complex settings and it is via this method that complexity can be defined and understood. Table 4 (below) outlines the goals and parameters for the two methods.

TABLE 4 *Qualitative and Quantitative Research*

Research Focus	Qualitative Research	Quantitative Research
Question	Why?	How Many and How Much?
Potential Goals	Both Formative and Summative: • informs design decisions; • helps identify usability issues and determines solutions	Mostly Summative: • evaluate the usability of an existing SMBC; • compare ROI
What Are the Outcomes?	Findings are based on the researcher's analysis, interpretations and prior knowledge	Statistical meaningful results that are likely to be replicated in another study
Methodology	• Limited participants • Flexible study conditions that can be adapted	• Many participants • Well-defined, controlled conditions

As the focus of this book looks at how social media consumer engagement can be used by brands to develop trust and build brand reputation with potential and current customers, the qualitative method can be used to explain the complexities involved and comprehend the social media setting as described by the multiple voices of brands, consumers and customers. As previously stated, there is no definitive approach to brand social media research and the positivist quantitative approach can be very effective for providing strategic insight. However, in order to further understand consumers' motivations to engage with a brand there are a number of qualitative methods that your organization can undertake to gain further insight into consumer trust development, which will be discussed throughout the remainder of this section. With this approach we can look at how to formulate a brand social media research strategy, looking at some of the methods and analysis options available.

SMBC qualitative research methods

Netnography

One such qualitative research method that you could undertake is a 'Netnography', which is an online research method derived from 'ethnography' and is a way of understanding social interaction in contemporary digital communications contexts. Ethnography is a research process in which the ethnographer (researcher) closely observes, records and engages in the daily life of another culture and then writes an account of this culture, emphasizing descriptive detail. The concept of netnography is credited to Robert V. Kozinets, a globally-recognized expert on social media, marketing research and branding. The netnography process is undertaken in digital environments, mostly online, and is defined as a specific set of research practices related to data collection, analysis, research ethics and representation that is rooted in participant observation. When a netnography is carried out, a considerable amount of the data originates in and manifests through the digital traces of naturally occurring public conversations, which are recorded by contemporary communications networks, such as social media platforms.

A netnography uses these conversations as data and highlights key themes and emerging trends. Essentially, it is an interpretive research method that adapts the traditional, in-person participant observation techniques of anthropology to the study of interactions and experiences occurring within digital platforms. It is increasingly recognized among marketing practitioners and brands alike that online communities or SMBCs connected to market-related topics can form suitable research environments containing detailed descriptions about the way consumers behave.

One of the main advantages of a netnography is that it is 'consumer-centric', allowing small, large or even global businesses to continually enhance their consumer and industry knowledge. A netnography also enables brands to gain an insight into how the consumer co-creation of value influences product development online. As a result of this method, organizations are able to use iterative process conceptualizations to explain the phenomena within the set context, allowing new theory and insights to emerge. Which makes netnography an ideal method to further investigate the brand trust development for your organization.

Case study approach

Another effective qualitative method is the use of case studies. A case study is typically regarded as a specific and bounded (in a time and place) instance of a phenomenon selected for study and the phenomenon of interest may be a person, process, event, group or organization. A key challenge and the biggest change associated with the advent of research in a social media environment is the potential to collect and review large datasets. The phrase 'Big data' is a term that describes a large volume of data (structured and unstructured) that inundates a business on a daily basis. But it's not the amount of data that's important, it's what your organization does with the data that matters and how it can be used to improve your operations.

Case studies provide a suitable brand research strategy for a number of key reasons: the researcher can study various aspects of brand perception, performance and comparison, learn about 'state-of-the-art' developments and generate theories from practice. Cases also allow brands to answer 'how' and 'why' questions in order to understand the nature and complexity of business life and provide an appropriate strategy to explore areas which require deeper understanding, such as how consumer trust is formed and developed. Using this approach allows your organization to learn about current industry activity and also generate theories from practice.

The tricky aspect when carrying out case study research is how reflective the findings are for your target audience in the sense that you could be making a 'generalization' about your findings. Research generalization is crucial in positivist research to determine how closely research findings can be applied with a specific level of statistical significance (i.e. worthy of attention or importance) to a wider population. There is an argument of course that generalizability should be addressed in all research since consideration of generalization can add rigour to any research findings and case study research has been criticized by some brand researchers who believe that they provide a limited basis for scientific generalization. However, some market researchers stress that generalizability is not an issue within qualitative research as the specificity of qualitative research virtually excludes generalizability and so it's not an issue for SMBC brand research, which uses this approach. Analytic generalization enables the researcher to expand and generalize theories rather than calculate frequencies, whereas statistical generalization is the process most common to positivist studies.

Validity and credibility of social media research

The next considerations for your research approach are the concepts of validity and credibility. These concepts have developed historically from previous research as a reflection of reality to the more astute view of knowledge as a 'social construction' of reality whereas positivist methods are predominantly concerned with ensuring results provide accurate reflections of reality. Validity is affected by the researcher's perception of validity in the study and their choice of a research approach. Consequently, researchers have developed their own concepts of validity and have adopted what they consider to be more appropriate terms, such as quality, rigour and trustworthiness.

To ensure credibility in the validation of social construction studies, researchers should employ one of three options: negative evidence (to explore multiple perspectives), engagement in the field (where multiple perspectives build 'context') or a thick, rich description (where vivid detail builds 'credibility'). From a social constructionist perspective, validity and credibility are present where findings 'reflect the phenomena of interest', i.e. that the research investigates what it sets out to explore. The theories, models and concepts you discover through your research will provide an understanding of a social context from a given perspective and the credibility of your research is achieved through something called 'theoretical saturation'. Theoretical saturation can be defined as the diminishing marginal contribution of each additional case, which essentially means there is no need to review additional data sets as no further insight is being presented. Once the data is 'saturated', you will be able to establish appropriate themes or categories which are built on rich, detailed consumer accounts.

In qualitative brand research, multi-method approaches are often employed by organizations to ensure the generalizability of the research and to enhance its reliability and validity. Using this approach can also reduce researcher bias if the researcher spends enough time in the field and employs multiple data collection strategies to corroborate findings. Time and resource are always the main considerations when deciding how to conduct research but by engaging in multiple methods, such as observation, interviews and recordings, your findings are likely to be more valid and reliable as they will incorporate a diverse construction of realities or different opinions or viewpoints from the data.

Reliability and validity can indicate trustworthiness, rigour and quality, which must be applied to all qualitative research so for instance if you decide to carry out interviews through social media as part of your study, consider the credibility of those being interviewed. Ask yourself questions when determining the interview sample which go alongside the research objectives. For instance, you may be keen to investigate why customers have stayed engaged with your SMBC in which case review whether interview participants have had a long or short history with your SMBC so that you have credible participants who will provide different perspectives. If you decide to focus on one area of qualitative study or would like to increase the validity by using multiple methods, the next step is to develop and determine your research design.

Research design

Your research design should act as the framework for collection and analysis of data which will help meet your objectives. Essentially, it is the logical approach that you will take to link the research question(s) and any issues with data collection, analysis and interpretation of findings in a clear and coherent way. To best illustrate an approach to research design we will review a multiple method approach and look at the key considerations. By incorporating a netnography, case studies and interviews you will be able to understand considerations for each element, should you just in turn decide to focus on one method for your research.

Multiple method research design

When carrying out SMBC research, your fieldwork can be conducted in six stages:

1   Sampling (i.e. identifying and tracking competitor communities to select highly social media active cases) and identifying consumers and organization experts (native speakers) for interview to discuss social media strategies of chosen cases.

2   Case study strategy (detailed investigation, with data collected over a period of time), the aim being to provide an analysis of the context and processes which illuminate the theoretical issues being investigated.

3   Social media netnography analysis of organizations' and competitors' SMBCs.

4   Consumer interview design or analysis (in order to generate themes for interviews).

5   Key informant interview design/analysis. Discussion of social media strategy and anticipated or resultant consumer responses by social media practitioners (interviews).

6   Analysis and conceptual framework development.

The research design for this approach involves a qualitative multiple case design, utilizing SMBCs, consumer in-depth interviews, as well as your own employees to serve as brand experts (key informants) in-depth interviews (telephone/face-to-face/social media). It could then adopt a thematic analysis approach (we'll cover this in more detail in the next section) to understand how social media consumer engagement can be used by brands to develop trust and build brand reputation with new and existing customers. Given the qualitative and inductive nature of this type of research approach, the key is to look for a convergence of themes and findings in order to develop meaningful, applicable conceptual framework conclusions to inform your brand strategy.

Key informants sampling

Let's start at the beginning: who are you going to analyse and talk to in order to give you the most effective results? Before we evaluate the most suitable option let's look at the four broad approaches to selecting a sample for a qualitative study:

- **Random sampling** – The principle of simple random sampling is that every object has the same probability of being chosen;
- **Convenience sampling** – Viewed as the least rigorous technique, this process involves the selection of the most accessible subjects to the researcher. It has many attractions, among them being the least costly to the researcher in terms of time, effort and money. However, there may be issues around the quality of data and intellectual credibility.
- **Purposive sampling** – Also referred to as 'judgemental sampling'. This is the most common sampling technique. Here, the researcher actively selects the most productive sample to answer the research question often based on the development of a framework of variables that might influence an individual's contribution.

- **Theoretical sampling** – This form of sampling is the iterative process of qualitative study design, where samples are usually theory driven to a greater or lesser extent. Theoretical sampling necessitates building interpretative theories from the emerging data and selecting a new sample to examine and elaborate on this theory.

When identifying key informants, sampling members with a specialist experience base provides credibility to qualitative studies because a greater depth of knowledge and understanding may be drawn upon from the data. Therefore, it is crucial to reflect on previous SMBC activity as well as examining the history of competitor brands researched, their social media engagement activity, the knowledge base of the key informants (employees) and the profile of consumers being researched. This then provides an understanding of the level of experience, engagement and membership participation within your chosen sample.

At this point it's worth highlighting a great quote from business researcher Evert Gummesson, who stated in his 2001 paper 'Are current research approaches in marketing leading us astray?', 'There is a wealth of information stored in the minds of people who have lived through important events with unique access.' This quote is not only applicable to your target audience or customers but also employees or individuals responsible for your brand. Employees have strong and holistic insight into strategies for their clients so they are holders of expert knowledge across functional areas of engagement with customers. When conducting qualitative research, the random sampling techniques used for quantitative studies are rarely appropriate. The process of selecting a random sample is well defined and rigorous and can be considered inappropriate for most qualitative research, specifically because the aim of a random sample is to provide the best opportunity to generalize the results to a population.

Random sampling can be effective for research, but it is not the most effective way of developing an understanding of complex social issues relating to human behaviour for both theoretical and practical reasons. The reasons are outlined below:

1 Samples for qualitative investigations are usually small. Even if a representative sample is suitable, the sampling error of such a small sample is likely to be so large that biases are inevitable.

2 For a true random sample to be selected, the characteristics under study of the whole population need to be known; this is rarely possible in a complex, qualitative study.

3 Random sampling of a population is likely to produce a representative sample only if the research characteristics are normally distributed within the population. The values, beliefs and attitudes that form the basis of qualitative investigation do not necessarily conform, making the probability approach inappropriate.

4 Individuals are not equally good at observing, understanding and interpreting their own and other people's behaviour. Qualitative researchers often recognize that some informants are 'richer' than others and these people are more likely to provide insights for the researcher.

So, it's fair to say random sampling may not be suitable for this type of research so let's focus on the alternative options to consider the most appropriate sample for your research.

Sampling schemes – generalization

For qualitative research, there are generally two types of statistical generalizations: external and internal. External statistical generalization, which is identical to the traditional notion of statistical generalization in quantitative research, concerns the creation of generalizations or inferences on data taken from a representative statistical sample of the population on which the sample was drawn. In contrast, internal statistical generalization involves making generalizations or inferences on data extracted from one or more representatives or elite participants about the sample from which the participants were drawn. Analytic generalizations are applied to wider theory on the basis of how selected cases 'fit' with the research issue. Social constructionist research studies phenomena (in this case, trust development through engagement) within their natural settings and attempts to make sense of, or to interpret, phenomena with respect to the meanings people bring.

The aim for your SMBC research is not to generalize to a population but to obtain insights into a phenomenon, individuals or events. As is most often the case in interpretivist studies, the qualitative researcher purposefully selects individuals, groups and settings for this phase to increase understanding of the phenomena under study. This approach gives you the flexibility to determine who and what you want to investigate for your organization. Again, this is not exactly easy but in general, sample sizes in qualitative research should not be so large that it is difficult to extract rich and varied data. On the other hand, the sample should also not be so small that it is hard to achieve data saturation or theoretical saturation.

When carrying out the netnography, a useful starting point for determining your sample is to look at your competitors or consider the organizations you aspire to be. Namely, who are you benchmarking your brand against?

Netnography research strategy

Benchmarking an organization's activity allows you to gain valuable insight into the successful strategies that your competitors or rivals use to maintain their market share. An effective method of benchmarking is to analyse these strategies as case studies and analyse their social media approach. Case study research for reviewing competitors' social channels consists of a thorough investigation, often with data collected over a period of time, of phenomena, within a set context. The aim is to provide an analysis of the context and processes which illuminate the issues being investigated, such as what platforms do they use to reach audiences, what content do they promote to create trust?

Furthermore, it is important to consider whether the case study will be exploratory (intended to research the problem but does not offer final and conclusive solutions), descriptive (used to describe characteristics of a population or phenomenon being studied) or explanatory (attempts to connect ideas to understand cause and effect) and a key decision to be made is whether the research will be based on a single case study or on multiple cases. Again, this can be based on your position in the market or the nuances of the industry you operate in.

The case study strategy is ideally suited to exploration of issues in depth and in following, leads into new areas of new constructions of theory.

Selecting data for the case study

A quick scan of your social media channels as well as those of your competitors will show you just how much data is available for social media research, which can be really off-putting and daunting for organizations of any size. In order to mitigate this issue, brands can focus on the concepts of 'central texts' and 'less central texts'. Research into building social media theory from case studies carried out by Professor Cathy Urquhart and Emmanuelle Vaast (2012) put forward the idea of 'central texts' and 'less central texts' and how these texts should be analysed. They advocate the method of analysing some text more deeply than others, hence the idea of having central texts to analyse. Less central texts can be used to provide corroboration and effectively back up or support the key themes. The logic of determining central texts provides an avenue for you to consider which data sources are important for your research. The argument for central and less central texts to be identified supports the idea of establishing the boundary of a case study. A further important consideration for your research is whether your boundary is purely a social media boundary, i.e. does the study only consider social media brand communities when collecting data? Or does it consider other digital discussion areas such as forums (as an example)? As discussed earlier, a further challenge when researching SMBCs is the context issue. If the research is confined to an online environment, the same argument for context is applicable.

Let's use Twitter as an example for conducting a netnography exercise. Investigating Twitter accounts in various contexts and situations would involve the selection of Tweets as the unit of analysis. However, in order to contextualize the study, Tweets are short, and making sense of the sentiment in itself is difficult as Tweets are to be understood within an ensemble, such as the notion of ambient awareness – i.e. an awareness created through regular and constant contact or exchange of information fragments through social media communities. For your own research, it is crucial that you consider context – i.e. what the organization tweeted and what were the responses involved. When digital texts embed links to other digital texts that have some conceptual relevance this again creates an issue in terms of the boundaries for the case study. An obvious downside is that you may feel totally overwhelmed by all this potentially relevant data. It might also be argued that, link by link, the entire Internet could become a research setting, making theory building all but impossible and meaningless. This example again emphasizes the requirement to set boundaries for the case companies being researched, suggesting purposeful sampling of similar groups that have different memberships can potentially increase the scope of the theory or the density of concepts that you develop.

TABLE 5 *Central and Less Central Digital Media Texts Characteristic*

Characteristic	Example	Text (Central or Less Central)
Held in digital format	Chat threads, photos	Central
Contained on a web site	Web content	Less
Co-produced by more than one person	Web forums, wikis	Less
Ephemeral	Comments on a link, Facebook post	Central
Embeds other discourses	Link within a web page, linking digital text to another	Less
Contains images	Avatar, web content, photos	Central
Contains video	YouTube clips	Central
Lack of context	Microblog posts, e.g. tweets 140 characters	Central
Linguistic innovations blurring the distinction between icons and discourse	Emoticons, acronyms, e.g. lol	Less

Source: Urquhart and Vaast (2012)

Case study boundaries and context

To help set your boundaries and context Table 5 – referenced in Urquhart and Vaast's research – categorizes texts which will help define and determine which aspects of social media communications you can investigate.

Possibilities and challenges monitoring SMBCs

Using a netnography has a number of advantages over traditional qualitative methods used to study the drivers of consumer behaviour – for instance, focus groups and market-orientated ethnographies. By investigating competitor social communities, as well as your own, you will be able to observe a natural information exchange that influences opinion among community members and listen in on how they talk about your brand's products or services. The community can also be observed without any invasion of privacy or interference in its activity. Of course, focus groups, personal interviews and traditional ethnographies have numerous benefits but they cannot be conducted unobtrusively, whereas a netnography can be conducted entirely unobtrusively, if so desired. We've mentioned that time and resource can be a factor for conducting your own brand research but using this approach lets you conduct extensive research at any time of day and all from the comfort of your own desk.

So in contrast to traditional ethnographies of consumer communities, online community research and social media research are less time-consuming and costly due to having continuous access to your informants. However, there are also challenges to using netnography. There is a large amount of data online, rendering these communities and their correspondence highly accessible to any researcher with access to the Internet. Considering the amount of information online, the main challenge for any netnography research you undertake is to find the relevant information about a research phenomenon and interpret it.

One further challenge is that netnography is also limited by the textual nature of a great deal of the communicative exchange, which misses much of the richness of in-person communication, such as tonal shifts, body language, eye movements and so on. Within a textual reality, the anonymity that is sometimes advantageous for obtaining disclosure could undermine your confidence in the information you are analysing. In other words, the researcher has no fully reliable means of verifying the participants' expertise or background. However, while you may not know the real people behind the people online, you can still understand how they behave, interact and construct their lives and realities online.

Constructing theory from social media research

Constructing theory from social media environments provides brands with significant challenges, such as theorizing both the source of the data and being mindful of the social material context. The case study method affords researchers the ability to adjust to the specifics of the environment and gradually get to collect multiple types of data. The label 'case study method' is a collective term, which indicates that developing a case study can rely upon a number of sources of evidence, such as documents, records and participant observation. This is particularly well suited to the purpose of generating theories using social media as these environments have the potential to generate new data and instil a need for creativity on the researchers' part regarding data collection and analysis. However, a key challenge facing researchers is analysing digital texts within social media environments.

Digital texts for SMBCs

A further challenge you may face while carrying out your research is defining legitimate units of analysis when in a social media environment as you are provided with a considerable amount of data (such as likes, posts and comments) that require evaluation. There is also the frequent use of imagery in nearly all brand social media communications, which should also be included as part of your qualitative research. However, Urquhart and Vaast's research (2012) highlighted that images tend to be analysed separately as opposed to being seen as part of the text that contains an image. They have also recommended that when reviewing digital text, images (with or without accompanying text) should be included. The characteristics of digital texts have been tabulated by them and are reviewed below in Table 6.

TABLE 6 *Characteristics of Digital Texts*

Characteristic	Context	Example
Held in digital format	The digital format characteristic aligns with the digital text definition, describing text that is held in a digital format. There are a number of examples that can create research concerns around data management.	Chat threads, photos
Contained a web site	The web site characteristic concerns the context in terms of what the web content actually provides for the consumer.	Web content
Co-produced by more than one person	Co-produced by more than one person; confronts researchers' ethical considerations within the research, such as letting the forum participants know that they are part of a research project, and does this require permission?	Web forums, wikis
Ephemeral	The ephemeral nature of the text creates further issues for social media research. This involves the creation of a systematic method of capturing texts. This, inevitably, can lead to the collection of large amounts of data, which effectively leads to further issues, such as data management and critically determining which texts are required for analysis.	Comments on a link, Facebook post
Embeds in other discourses	Digital texts can often embed other texts using hyperlinks. A key aspect of a digital environment is the potential to link content to each other. Hence, datal texts can embedded in each another, creating new issues for data collection.	Link within a web page, linking digital text to another
Contains images	Imagery within social media is also an important characteristic to consider due to its popularity in newer social media platforms, such as Instagram and Pinterest.	Avatar, web content, photos
Contains video	Video content supports the previous characteristic. Information videos provide information from nonverbal cues. As a result, social media research may ascertain a lot information from such video sources and they should be considered when designing the study.	YouTube clips
Lack context	Lack of context is a consideration that social media researchers should also be aware of, such as time of day or ccmpany background.	Microblog posts, e.g. Tweets 140 characters
Linguistic innovations blurring the distinction between icons and discourse	Linguistic innovations encompass the growing dependence upon acronyms, such as 'LOL', 'FYI'. Furthermore they have transformed written text, making it in some ways closer to oral language, like when lol interrupts a digital conversation, similarty to when laughter punctuates an unmediated conversation (Spencer and Mandelli. 2007).	Emoticons, acronyms

Source: Urquhart and Vaast (2012)

Data analysis

Once all the considerations have been factored into your design, you can determine the cases under consideration, the units you will measure and the time you will spend carrying out the netnography. The next hurdle is determining how you are going to analyse the data. Data are, by definition, raw intelligence that requires analysis and subsequent interpretation to become useful information. Effective analysis of any research activity aims to provide sense, reduce volume and identify trends and themes which allow you to construct a framework for communicating the essence of what the data reveals. There are several generally accepted methods of analysing qualitative data, as outlined in Table 7.

Qualitative thematic content analysis

Code-book analysis, also referred to as 'qualitative thematic content analysis', falls within the social construction framework which involves data analysis based on a thematic (coding) template and

TABLE 7 *Qualitative Data Analysis Methods*

Discourse analysis	Interpreting language used by individuals within a specific social context
Narrative analysis	Showcasing the stories and metaphors that people tell and use to interpret their lives and the social context of the world around them
Thematic Content analysis	The classification of textual units into specific categories for identification of inferences around a specific social phenomenon
Template analysis	Interpretation through the design of a template consisting of codes subject to continual review and change as the researcher gathers and analyses data in order to highlight themes and patterns within the data

Source: Bryman and Bell (2007)

this is the approach which could be most suitable for brand research on social media. Digressions and repetitions are edited out of social media category postings and transcript excerpts for reasons of brevity and ease of understanding. However, any case study within qualitative research should by its very nature be flexible and open, and as a consequence may continue to evolve throughout your research. As a result, any social media posts can be analysed and transcribed on an ongoing basis and it is also an idea to have accompanying brief field notes so that any emergent phenomena can be probed in any follow-up interviews.

You may be really confident that any form of social research you carry out will fulfil certain quality criteria for measuring and collecting data. Nevertheless, it is widely accepted that measurement or the methods of measurement should be as objective, reliable and valid as possible. When conducting content analysis, the research strategy often undertaken is governed by the traditional criteria of validity and reliability, where the latter is a precondition for the former (but not vice versa). Since arguments concerning the content can be viewed to be more important than methodical issues in qualitative analysis, validity takes priority over reliability.

Data collection application

OK, so how do you then go about collecting your netnography data? The social constructionist paradigm, inductive method and qualitative data gathering approaches are all focused on giving a voice to the reality perceived by individuals to a given social phenomena and specific contexts. To accomplish this, you can use a number of interpretive techniques to describe and then decode the messages received from the study. According to netnography principles, data collection and analysis require joining and actively participating in the communities under study to become familiar with the context and cultural aspects of the communities. Thematic frameworks are often used to then analyse qualitative data and data collected using a netnography can be effectively analysed using thematic content analysis. Thematic content analysis is one of the main procedures for analysing textual material, no matter where the material comes from – ranging from consumer interviews to e-WOM discussions on your SMBC. One of the essential features is the use of categories which are repeatedly assessed and modified, if required.

Analysis framework

The analysis for this approach involves exploring data for themes, constructs and patterns with the inclusion of quotations from consumer posts or comments, which are then used to describe and explain phenomena. The analysis is then an ongoing iterative process, which requires reading and re-evaluating transcripts to ascertain a comprehensive understanding of the data and its underlying themes across cases. Initial conceptualizations from pilot research can then structure and steer data gathering and analysis through emergent themes that arise. Conclusions can then be drawn from the data, with comparisons being made from the data sources.

Coding and template analysis allow textual analysis to be conducted from the netnography case studies and interview transcripts. Themes from the data can then be highlighted and coded to attain higher order themes. Theoretical saturation can then be achieved through the evidence of recurrent themes across cases. There are also various ways of analysing visual data such as images, photos and videos. First, the information can be coded as if it was any other type of digital text. Most qualitative data analysis packages have the capability to store visuals and code themes; hence, there seems to be no obstacle to this type of analysis being conducted. A thematic analysis framework is presented in Figure 20 (below).

This structure should facilitate the fluidity of movement as it allows the sub-groups and codes to influence emergent themes. Critics of this approach might question the suggested structure and organization of a project as time-consuming and unnecessary. However, as mentioned previously, this can be considered to be data familiarization, which can lead to your brand research generating initial codes, searching for themes, reviewing themes, defining themes and producing findings. An on-going reflexivity (your awareness of an analytic focus on your relationship to the field of study) method should also increase the validity and credibility of the study. Figure 21 (page 200) highlights a potential analytical framework you could adopt when reviewing each social media post in order to categorize and analyse emergent themes.

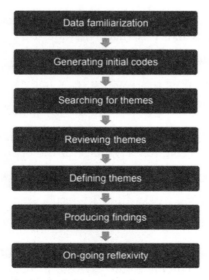

FIGURE 20 *Thematic Analysis Framework*

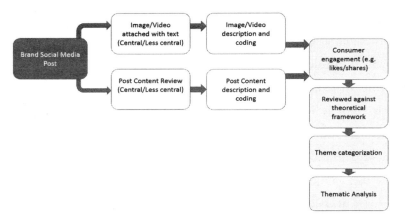

FIGURE 21 *Social Media Netnography Analytical Framework*

Interviews

As previously discussed, in order to add further validity to your research you can reinforce your netnography findings using SMBC platforms to conduct follow-up interviews. In-depth interviews are a significant source of evidence used for brand research as they are one of the most powerful tools in a qualitative methodology, with the capability of deriving shared meanings for brands and consumers. They are also considered to be one of the best methods of gathering detailed information and are one of the most common and powerful ways to truly understand consumer and employee opinion. By adopting a guided interview approach, the in-depth method also has the advantage that issues are framed by participants and are designed to take full advantage of the opportunity of gaining new insight. However, a key concern you must be wary of for in-depth research is that individuals lead hectic, deeply segmented and privacy-centred lives, so even the most willing participants may only have limited time and availability. Consequently, time issues and concerns regarding privacy can be important impediments to the qualitative study of modern life and this may also be the case when interviewing key informants and consumers so when planning your interviews, ensure they are co-ordinated at convenient times for all participants. The rationale for utilizing the in-depth interview method in social construction research is that interviews act as interactions that lead to contextually based results, which are able to reveal both the 'how' and the 'what' of consumer opinion for your brand.

Elicitation, probing and laddering

Elicitation and probing allow interviewees to report with a fair degree of accuracy the perceptions, judgements, decisions and particular areas of experience of individuals. From a social constructionist perspective, elicitation techniques should have an exploratory emergent character implicit in the process of revealing tacit or subjective understandings. Consequently, the interview guidelines you compose should be open and flexible to accommodate new phenomena and exploration of themes. A key advantage of this method is that utilizing open questions allows your interviewees to speak freely about complex issues, which would have been difficult to determine from alternative approaches such as a closed-questionnaire. This also allows respondents to determine their own answers, so not limiting possible new insights.

The interview techniques undertaken for each interview should always include clarification, feedback (without leading the interviewee) and probing. This approach ensures that questions and answers are understood, participants are encouraged to share experiences and deeper meanings are investigated via 'laddering' to provide full, rich and comprehensive data for analysis. Laddering allows the researcher to understand an individual's mindset where 'laddering up' provides information as to why a particular aspect is important and 'laddering

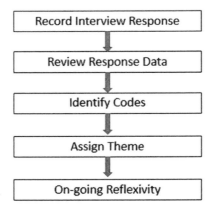

FIGURE 22 *Interview Framework*

down' explores the effect of perceptions. Figure 22 highlights a potential framework that could be used when conducting and analysing interview responses.

The interview transcripts alongside the netnography findings can then be analysed to identify the constructs that form part of your research question. Constructs can then be tabulated and a qualitative thematic analysis conducted to categorize the activity and eventually develop a conceptual model.

Conceptual models

From a conceptual viewpoint, a framework is required which allows you to better understand the research area you are investigating. Conceptual models are visual displays of theory (represented in Chapter 3) demonstrating a picture of what the theory says is going on with the phenomenon being investigated. The book *Qualitative Analysis* (1994) by Miles and Huberman defined a conceptual model as a visual or written product that 'explains, either graphically or in narrative form, the main things to be studied, the key factors, concepts, or variables, and the presumed relationships among them'. A conceptual model consists of two things: concepts and their relationships (Miles and Huberman, 1994) and can be used to pull together theory in order to see its implications, limitations and relevance to research. They can also be used to develop theory, assisting you by identifying unexpected connections, or to highlight holes or contradictions in your current strategy and develop methods to resolve these issues in practice.

Conceptual frameworks are best suited to studies of social processes and the conceptual framework is not an end in itself, it is a tool for developing theory and making that theory more explicit. A conceptual model is not something you do once and are finished with, your organization should go back and rework frameworks as understanding of the phenomena being investigated develops. Consequently, each iteration of the model presented can be used to inform the next stage of the research, as well as any updates as a result of additional findings.

Conceptual framework development

For conceptual framework development, data is analysed in order to conceptually develop an understanding of the area under investigation. Aspects are then identified and incorporated into the previous analysis findings to create the final stage of the conceptual model. Findings are then conceptually developed and, as Gummesson ('Qualitative research in marketing', *European Journal of Marketing*, 2005) stated with regard to qualitative research, if the aim is theory generation then the study must provide conceptualization and condensation or the researcher has not provided an interpretation or meaning to the phenomena.

Driving your research findings constructs

The final stage concerns reviewing the constructs that have helped investigate your research issues. Once transcripts have been analysed and thematically coded, core constructs can then be outlined and a comparative thematic matrix analysis of the transcripts can be developed to display the prevalence of each theme. Themes may then be positioned into concepts, which are examined in order to determine what is affecting the phenomena. Based on the overall prevalence of each theme across cases, a hierarchy of concepts can then be developed. Categories are then able to be utilized to organize the data and determine the nature of the constructs and any relationships between them. Concepts which emerge from a netnography and interviews can then be compared with existing and emergent themes from previous strategic frameworks to contrast or confirm existing theories, as well as contributing new strategic methods. The findings can then be conceptualized into a conceptual model, which will assist your social media strategy.

6

Bitcoin and Digital Trust

In 1999, Professor Milton Friedman, a Nobel Prize winner in economics, stated, 'I think the internet is going to be one of the major forces for reducing the role of government. The one thing that's missing, but that will soon be developed, is a reliable e-cash.' Nine years later, Bitcoin was born, allegedly created by a programmer called Satoshi Nakamoto (although the true identity of Bitcoin's creator is unclear). The motivation behind the design and development of the digital currency and its software was to utilize the Internet to establish a form of peer-to-peer electronic cash system. Bitcoin has been described, by advocates, as 'the internet of money' or 'the first online currency based on highly distributed trust', but how do social media and trust affect Bitcoin?

Understanding the Bitcoin system can be very complicated so before we go into more details, I have updated an example first put forward by Nik Custodio, Senior Director, FTI Consulting/UX to give a basic overview of how Bitcoin works (from https://medium.com/free-code-camp/explain-bitcoin-like-im-five-73b4257ac833).

Imagine we're sitting in a coffee shop, I have a coffee but I give it to you. You now have a coffee and I don't. The coffee was physically placed into your hand. You saw me hand it to you and I saw you take it. We didn't need a third person such as a coffee shop barista there to help us make the transfer or indeed confirm that the coffee was passed to you. The coffee is now yours and I can't give you another coffee as I don't have any more money to buy one. So the coffee is in your hands now and you control what happens to it next, it's left my possession completely. If you saw a friend in the coffee shop you could give it to them and then they could pass it on and so on and so forth. This is basically what an in-person exchange involves.

But let's say I have a digital coffee and I give you my digital coffee, how do you know that the digital coffee which used to be mine is now yours, and yours alone? How do you know that I didn't send the digital coffee on to other people as well, like in an email attachment, or that I haven't made numerous copies of that digital coffee on my computer or uploaded it online so that anyone can download the coffee? So you realize that this digital exchange is a bit of an issue and sending digital coffees is not like sending physical coffees. There's actually a name for this issue called the double-spending problem, which is the risk that an individual could send a single unit of currency to two different sources at the same time.

So how could you keep track of the digital coffees I've sent you? Well, they could be tracked in a ledger. Which is basically a book where you can track all transactions. As this ledger is digital, it needs to live in its own world and have someone in charge of it. But this isn't the same as you and me in the coffee shop, as it was just the two of us then, using a ledger involves using a third party for our transactions, so we are looking for a way of replicating our experience from the coffee shop to a digital environment. But what if we gave the ledger to everyone and instead of the ledger being accessible on one computer, you could access it on everybody's computers. All the transactions that have ever happened, from all time, in digital coffees, will be recorded in it. Crucially, there are no more cheating options with this system. I can't send you digital coffees that I am not in possession of, because it wouldn't sync up with everybody else in the system. Also, the system is not controlled by one individual, so I know there's no one person that can just decide to give himself more digital coffees. The rules of the system were already defined at the beginning. The code and rules for this system are open source (denoting software for which the original source code is made freely available and may be redistributed and modified) and this is in place for smart people to maintain, secure, improve, and check.

But you can also participate in this network as well updating the ledger and making sure it all checks out. For your efforts you could receive a number of digital coffees as a reward. This is clearly a simplified version but this system is called the Bitcoin protocol and the digital coffees are the Bitcoins within the system. Having an 'open source' public ledger means that the total number of digital coffees is defined in the public ledger at the beginning so we know the exact amount that exists within the system and how limited they are. So now, when I make an exchange I now know that my digital coffee certifiably left my possession and is now completely yours. It will be updated and verified by the public ledger. Due to the fact that it is a public ledger we don't need an impartial third party to ensure that I didn't cheat, or make extra copies for myself, or send the digital coffee to other people as well. Within the system the exchange of a digital coffee is now exactly like the exchange of a physical one, just as if we were back in the shop. So we can now exchange as many coffees as we like anywhere in the world at any time.

Social media and cryptocurrency

As previously discussed, the impact that social media has had on a number of industries has been incredible, one such industry being cryptocurrency. A lot of the attention and interest in cryptocurrency has been attributed to social media promotion. The relationship between social media, cryptocurrency and Blockchain is certainly an exciting one. As business author Jonathan Hassell (2016) explains in digital magazine *CIO*, 'A blockchain is the structure of data that represents a financial ledger entry, or a record of a transaction. Each transaction is digitally signed to ensure its authenticity and that no one tampers with it, so the ledger itself and the existing transactions within it are assumed to be of high integrity.'

The technology used to develop cryptocurrency and Blockchain continues to evolve and social media plays an interesting role in this development by sharing the stories and promoting the potential. But first, let's look at what exactly cryptocurrency is, its relationship with social media and what the future may hold for developing trust with customers. Cryptocurrency has grown considerably in both value and popularity recently. Indeed, many high-profile and trusted brands support Blockchain cryptocurrency, such as Microsoft and JP Morgan Chase. However, this wasn't always the case. Less than a decade ago, Bitcoin was valued at just a few cents, but at the time of writing, one Bitcoin is worth US$3,723.85.

This is a pretty big shift in valuation so how did this change in value and popularity come about? Well, social media has had a huge influence on the success that cryptocurrency is currently experiencing. The buzz can be linked to a relatively low-profile digital forum called Bitcoin Talk in 2010, where Laszlo Hanyecz, a Florida-based programmer working for online retail company GoRuck, posted a potential Bitcoin transaction for two Papa John's pizzas. The pizzas were bought for 10,000 Bitcoins, which are worth millions today. This straightforward transaction has led to significant development and ever since that first-ever recorded transaction of Bitcoin for a physical good, the use of the currency has taken off, with customers now able to use Bitcoin for things like online shopping, airplane tickets and let's not forget, pizza. So began the relationship between cryptocurrency and social media. Social media platforms and other media outlets are able to significantly influence cryptocurrency price fluctuations, for better or for worse. But social media and forums are still essential for the growth of digital currency and Blockchain technology. As cryptocurrency growth continues, consumers and brands are more interested in using and investing in it.

The dynamics of the actual Bitcoin price can relate to important discussions and opinions posted on social media, where investors and business adopters interact and provide feedback about the market. Previous commentary has argued that social media and user-generated content (UGC) in particular constitute important determinants of investments for businesses and individuals. Social media channels are able to capture current opinion and provide low-cost platforms for connecting with target markets so Bitcoin essentially provides a unique opportunity for brands to observe, analyse and understand the interplay of social media with the value of a financial instrument.

As Bitcoin is the most popular virtual currency (other currencies include Litecoin and Zcash, for example), there is a fair assumption that it behaves similarly to traditional currencies, such as its price being driven by its use in transactions, supply and its price level for the trading of goods and services. However, Bitcoin is a vastly different financial phenomenon as the European Central Bank in its 2012 report 'Virtual Currency Schemes' described it as 'unregulated, digital money, which is issued and usually controlled by its developers and used and accepted among the members of a specific virtual community'. As Bitcoin is supported by a decentralized payment network, financial transactions are not denominated in dollars, pounds or in fact any other currency. Because the value of Bitcoin derives not from gold or government fiat (fiat money is a currency without intrinsic value that has been established as money, often by government regulation), its value is determined by those who assign to it so its monetary value is determined on an open market, similar to the exchange rate among world currencies. However, Bitcoin's daily exchange rates do not correlate with traditional currencies and its exchange rate volatility is analysed in orders of magnitude greater than the volatilities of those more widely used currencies. In this respect, bitcoin imitates the traits associated with Internet stock rather than currency.

Technically speaking, Bitcoin was an attempt to create a separate digital currency and payment system, making online transactions purely peer-to-peer without centralized mediation. Bitcoin does not reduce trust but rather shifts it, where essentially, the trust in banks or governments is transferred to trust in algorithms and encryption software. It does so by implementing cryptography as a means of verifying and securing online transactions. Bitcoin could easily be referred to as 'Bitchain' as Nakamoto (*Bitcoin: A Peer-to-Peer Electronic Cash System*, 2008) defines Bitcoin as 'a chain of digital signatures'. It has no physical quality, being nothing more than an entry on a digital register. When a digital transfer is carried out, the owner leaves an identifying signature validating legitimate acquisition of the coins and a unique public key for the next owner. The receiver can trace the attached signatures to 'verify the chain of ownership' (Nakamoto, 2008) and transactions are broadcasted and then 'timestamped' to prevent double spending.

External nodes, or individual central processing units (CPUs), create a peer-to-peer network that legitimizes transfers and stores this information in a block. This block then contains the transaction history with a complex mathematical algorithm. The nodes then subsequently compete to solve these algorithms and when successful, develop a new block – a process known as 'mining for coins'. The node that solves the algorithm wins a new Bitcoin and this is the incentive for both the maintenance of the network and the honesty of nodes. Using this anonymous and decentralized method, Bitcoin does not rely on a central authority or central node to disseminate and regulate currency. The actual network itself does this and maintains Bitcoin's nominal value.

Is Bitcoin useful for businesses?

There have also been slightly questionable claims regarding the potential of Bitcoin, with some commentators claiming it will completely replace our current established financial systems or that it is the future universal currency seen in science fiction films. However, there's no denying the potential for Bitcoin is very interesting and could challenge established financial systems. In spite of the criticisms Bitcoin is still an important consideration for businesses due to the technology that it is founded on. Bitcoin is founded on Blockchain computing and the impact that 'Blockchain' is having on businesses is similar to how the Internet changed traditional computer networks.

Blockchain computing

Blockchain computing is a system that can securely contain an entire set of records within it, which are classed as blocks. It is unique in that copies of the entire system can be kept simultaneously on millions of computers located anywhere in the world. Blockchain technology eradicates the idea that information is stored in a finite number of locations and allows information to be held on multiple systems simultaneously. When a new entry is added to the Blockchain, the whole system instantly updates in every location. An unlimited number of copies of the entire system, updated right to the present moment, is maintained across the globe. A key benefit is that while any employee can add a new record to the system, changing or updating an old record would require the permission of each computer on which the data resides.

Blockchain and trust

One of the things that intermediaries such as banks, estate agents and traders rely on when collecting fees is their reputation for integrity. We trust online banking as we know when we transfer money online it will reach the correct account and there will be an accurate record of the transaction. However, if a transaction between an individual and a stranger could happen without using a bank or PayPal that was secure, some consumers may find this appealing. Blockchain provides this option as Blockchain records claim to always be accurate and trustworthy. This means that transactions can occur without the need for an intermediary to send and receive money. The key trust issue for users, however, would be: is Blockchain hackable? Well, from a practical perspective, Blockchain cannot be hacked. The records on all the many computers holding identical information are essentially interlocked so in theory if one computer's Blockchain updates are hacked, it will be rejected by the entire system. Changes can only be made if the countless sites where the Blockchain resides all agree to the same change, which in theory makes it un-hackable. However, nothing is completely impossible in today's technological environment and just as a bank's security systems can be hacked, so too could Blockchain's. The only way a system can be hacked would be if all the system locations in the world, possibly located on a vast number of computers, could be hacked simultaneously. It's possible in theory, but the undertaking would be so massive that only a government-scale effort could even contemplate it.

So how does digital trust fit into all this?

The Blockchain that is used is essentially displayed as an algorithmic tool to encourage trust, discounting usual trust measures such as trusted third parties or social capital, so the virtual currency which is issued and controlled by its developers can be used as legal tender. This process has created a new form of consumer trust. As Popper (*Digital Gold – Bitcoin and the Inside Story of the Misfits and Millionaires Trying to Reinvent Money*, 2015) states, 'The primary value the coins had was the expectation that they would be worth more in the future, allowing current holders to cash out for more than they paid.'

Should the trust and willingness of market participants to exchange fiat currency (currency that a government has declared to be legal tender, but is not backed by a physical commodity) for Bitcoin decline, this could result in the permanent loss of value of Bitcoin.

Bitcoin issues

Practical applications

Ironically, Bitcoin's current boom is making it very difficult to use as a currency. For example in 2017, the gaming company STEAM stopped accepting Bitcoin as a payment option, due to its volatility and high transaction fees (verge.com). As the price of Bitcoin fluctuates so drastically, it can literally increase as consumers go through the online checkout process. As a result, the company had to refund the difference back to customers, which incurred a transaction fee each time. The price hikes are great for those who have already invested in Bitcoin, but these issues highlight that Bitcoin is still some way away from being used for mainstream e-commerce.

Bitcoin – Psychological biases

Cryptocurrency is still seen as a thing of the future, but being aware of the emotional pitfalls connected to Bitcoin could potentially save your brand and consumers money. Relatively speaking, worldwide there is only a small part of the population that has invested in Bitcoin and the number of organizations accepting it as payment is limited. Plus, the stock market is erratic, peaking and crashing almost weekly, which does not inspire confidence. Furthermore, as touched upon earlier, the concept is difficult to understand, particularly for consumers who do not have a technological background. It's fair to say it is currently only used by those who not only understand the technology, but also understand the market. Nevertheless, there have been numerous promotional pieces extolling the benefits of Bitcoin, so naturally, consumers have an interest. To begin the learning process, we can use heuristics (quick-learning techniques) and analyse other people's behaviour to make decisions.

As consumers, we are not as rational as we might think. Our choices are fuelled by irrationality, heuristics and emotions – useful in daily life, but maybe not so much when learning to trade with Bitcoin. Interest in Bitcoin can start after listening to an inviting sales pitch, often being sold on the premise that 'you can't lose'. However, relying on these methods has many pitfalls, so before engaging in the world of cryptocurrency, it's important to consider the following psychological biases that are highly prominent.

Social proofing

We have discussed social proofing for consumer engagement previously, where social proof is a psychological phenomenon where people assume the actions of others in an effort to display correct behaviour for a given social situation. Social proofing is based on the notion of normative social influence, which argues that people will conform in order to be liked by, similar to or accepted by the influencer (or society). For example, when you 'like' a comment or Tweet from an industry expert you respect or admire, that's social proofing. In pure terms, social proofing uses third-party influence to alter an individual's mindset.

In most situations when we are unsure of what choice we need to make, we look to others for a clue or behaviour guideline. This particular heuristic trait is sometimes exploited by traders through a tactic called 'Shilling'. Shilling involves traders making it appear that many people will invest in a coin in order to generate demand. As cryptocurrency technology is highly complicated and many don't fully understand it, they will look for other cues to help them form a decision. One of those cues is to see how many others have invested in a certain area. This desire for social proof helps us to make daily decisions. However, when investing money in a cryptocurrency, it's important to consider more than just a pack mentality.

Key influencer/Authority

When researching a new topic, often we look to key influencers or those we are aware of who have an expertise in the area we are looking into, purely based on their reputation. In the case of Bitcoin, everyone was exposed to this new concept via all forms of media, which led to some confusion – potentially ideal for those looking to promote Bitcoin.

As consumers, we are often tempted to conform to what everyone around us seems to be doing. Extensive media coverage can heighten the feeling that we're missing out on something that everyone else is doing, and the more we hear about something like Bitcoin, the less risky it seems to us. Industry leaders such as Richard Branson and Peter Thiel have recently discussed the area:

'Well, I think it is working. There may be other currencies like it that may be even better. But in the meantime, there's a big industry around Bitcoin. People have made fortunes off Bitcoin, some have lost money. It is volatile, but people make money off of volatility too.'

Richard Branson, Virgin Group (source: Bitcoin.com, 2016)

'PayPal had these goals of creating a new currency. We failed at that, and we just created a new payment system. I think Bitcoin has succeeded on the level of a new currency, but the payment system is somewhat lacking. It's very hard to use, and that's the big challenge on the Bitcoin side.'

Peter Thiel, Co-Founder of PayPal (source: Cryptocoinnews, 2015)

To deal with this lack of context, consumers might be inclined to engage with someone who has (or promotes that they have) been very successful with Bitcoin. We are more likely to listen to someone who has status in a subject area as from an early age, we are conditioned to take all authority figures seriously. However, it's vital to bear in mind that even experienced authority figures are not right every time, especially in a market where technology updates are in a consistent state of flux.

Scarcity

There is also the 'scarcity' factor. Scarcity implies that opportunities appear more beneficial or valuable to people when availability is restricted or limited. After being influenced by social proof and key influencers, scarcity plays a significant role in influencing consumers to make purchases. In the case of Bitcoin, the more people who bought it, the more expensive it got. Since people were unaware of the apparent scarcity of Bitcoin, subsequently hearing about this scarcity made consumers eager to buy it as soon as possible.

Commitment and consistency

Humans have a near-obsessive desire to be and appear consistent with what we do. Once we make a decision and commit, often we pressurize ourselves to maintain the stance we have chosen, especially when any commitment we have made has been announced in a public domain. The desire for consistency is even stronger.

Inaction inertia

We are often exposed to deals but sometimes we hear about offers that we passed on, which we regret. This leads to a psychological state known as 'inaction inertia'. Inaction inertia is the state a person experiences after missing out on a deal, making them less likely to purchase the same product in the future for an increased price. Consumers are loath to miss out on bargains, but because of our nature, this is a psychological bias that can actually save us money. It can also diminish profits, especially in the world of cryptocurrencies. The first time you hear about a coin, its price may have increased by 50 per cent, then 100 per cent and then 200 per cent. This is when inaction inertia is overridden by a state called 'fear of missing out'.

Fear of missing out

Perhaps one of the most well-known psychological phenomena that is increasing interest in Bitcoin is the fear of missing out (FOMO). Successful Bitcoin investors greatly enjoy sharing their experiences, particularly how much money they have made. This leads to others feeling they can't miss out on such an opportunity and can lead to feelings of anxiety.

Confirmation bias

One further consideration before investing is the potential for confirmation bias. Confirmation bias is the tendency for individuals to seek out or prefer information that strengthens their theory or belief. If there are both positive and negative impacts connected to an investment, individuals are more likely to look at the positive remarks to confirm that they made the right decision.

UGC and Bitcoin

There have been a number of studies which have investigated how the Internet and influence of user-generated content (UGC) affect stock market behaviour, with mixed results. Some studies argue that daily posting volume is associated with both earnings announcement events and changes in stock trading volume and returns whereas others have found no significant predictive ability for individual stock returns using message board sentiment. For social media communities, opinion is divided, with arguments presented to say that views expressed in both articles and comments on a social media platform can predict future stock returns and earnings surprises, with an effect that is both statistically and economically significant whereas some findings suggest a 'positive shock' to message board postings can predict negative stock returns on the next day, though the effect is economically small.

While there is conflicting opinion regarding the impact of user-generated content on digital platforms, it is clear that online engagement and discussions offer strong indications of the general market sentiment towards Bitcoin. Therefore, user-generated content can have an effect on investment returns and the trading volume of Bitcoins for numerous reasons. For instance, one of the main motivations for early institutional Bitcoin adopters was to capitalize on positive public relations through social media and to be seen as an innovator. The social gaming organization Zynga did exactly this in 2014 when it added Bitcoin options to its games and received a lot of media coverage. Furthermore, due to the decentralized nature of Bitcoin most early users were individuals rather than large financial organizations. It might be argued that these early adopters are more active on social media and therefore more likely to be influenced by the content they view on these platforms.

The significant role of social influence in the Bitcoin market

For statistical analysis there is a term called a 'power law', which describes a functional relationship between two quantities whereby a relative change in one quantity results in a proportional relative change in the other, which is independent of the initial size of those quantities. Put simply, one quantity varies as a power of another. The concept of power law is applicable to user content on social media and implies that due to the huge numbers active against the amount of content posted, users provide little content or only contribute sporadically. When reviewing social influence it's important to consider the different groups active on social media, e.g. silent majority, vocal minority, as those groups have considerable differences when it comes to engaging online and generating content. Again, the foundation for influence is the decentralized nature of Bitcoin, which means most grassroots users can often be categorized as 'silent majority'. In this regard, the UGC from the silent majority may have been a more compelling metric for series investors.

Social media community members differ in terms of the frequency of visits, volume, type, as well as quality of digital content they generate and engage with. The effectiveness and functioning of a social media community is dependent on the presence and activities of a vocal minority of opinion leaders, who can influence activity in a number of ways. The same influence can also be applied to the Bitcoin market. The argument was recently endorsed by research led by Professor Feng Mai of Stevens Institute of Technology, New Jersey, whose 2018 paper 'How Does Social Media Impact Bitcoin Value? A Test of the Silent Majority Hypothesis' claimed that Bitcoin's value can indeed be manipulated by public sentiment, stating social media and Bitcoin prices are certainly linked. Remember our old friend Netnography? Mai adopted a netnography approach for their research. To give the findings credibility, the study collected and analysed two years' worth of comments on Bitcointalk, one of the world's most popular Bitcoin forums. The analysis approach involved classifying comments into positive, negative and other sentiment categories using natural-language processing techniques. They also collected two months' worth of Twitter data, which included more than 3.4 million Tweets about Bitcoin. It's fair to say this was a large and representative sample.

The analysis then compared changes in Bitcoin's price with the comments around the cryptocurrency. However, just as the comments can impact on the price, Bitcoin's value can affect the sentiment around it, so the analysts also considered daily rises and falls in indicators such as the S&P 500 stock index, gold prices and volatility indexes to further understand the correlation. To gain further insight, the research team also categorized Bitcoin tweeters and posters into two different groups. Namely, frequent and infrequent posters to determine what types of commenters affect prices the most.

The findings indicated that sustained periods of increasingly positive social media commentary do, in fact, considerably influence the rising price of Bitcoin. Surprisingly though it was the silent majority, not the vocal minority, who move these prices. So basically, it wasn't the Facebook comments from active users that affected price, it was the infrequent users who took the time to comment on the cryptocurrency's prospects that impacted prices tenfold if they left positive comments. So why did this happen as it certainly wasn't expected? Well, interestingly, they found that the price instead changed in proportion to the comments made by infrequent posters, the main cause being that frequent users are often perceived as having an agenda by fellow community members – in this instance hyping the price of Bitcoin because they themselves had invested in it. Therefore, as Professor Mai concluded, if the majority of the posts around Bitcoin are generated by people who are biased, the sentiments on social media may not accurately reflect the currency's actual value. Finally, the research argued that Bitcoin investors recognize these potential conflicts of interest and therefore discount them. As Professor Mai stated, 'The silent majority are the real influencers in driving the value of Bitcoin. It seems like investors get that.'

What does the future hold?

It's hard to deny that social media has played a huge role in boosting cryptocurrency's profile. Global brands are now taking a strong look at cryptocurrency and Blockchain technology to streamline many of their current, often antiquated operational processes. Crypto-based social platforms are evolving and offer solutions to many of the issues traditional social networks have in place for both consumers and brands. A Blockchain-based social media decentralized network with no central server could give consumers decentralized social content, which would effectively give control to the users and the content they decide to post so basically there would be no more adherence to the rules or algorithms of Facebook.

Using crypto-based social channels could also mean increased security for users as they can allow users to maintain their personal and online data habits. Transactions could also become far more streamlined. Consumer transactions that happen over social media can be time-consuming as there are only a limited number of ways to make payments. A crypto-based social platform could potentially change all that as consumers will have more ways to pay, with each method being extremely secure. This means that your brand could develop better leads and obtain more consumer data using Basic Attention Token (BAT) processes. The Basic Attention Token is an example of how Blockchain technology and cryptocurrency are impacting established social media strategies and practices due to ad blocking. In the future brands may move away from platforms such as Facebook to deliver target adverts to consumers and instead go straight to users to get more accurate consumer data. As a result, consumers have more control and are rewarded with BAT tokens for their data and viewing preferences. One example of an organization adopting this approach is Steemit (not to be confused with the gaming company STEAM).

Steemit is a blogging and social networking website owned by Steemit, Inc., which uses the Steem Blockchain to reward publishers and curators. It was founded by Ned Scott and Dan Larimer, creator of BitShares, and EOS in 2016. Signing up is free and there are no hidden costs or ads on the site, which is seen as a fresh alternative to social media giants like Facebook or Twitter. Steemit has had the first mover advantage and is currently seen as *the* Blockchain social media platform.

On Steemit, users can upvote posts and comments similar to other blogging websites or social news websites like Reddit and the authors who get upvoted receive a monetary reward in a cryptocurrency token named 'Steem' and US dollar-pegged tokens called 'Steem Dollars'. On Reddit, upvotes provide greater visibility and even the chance of landing on the front page. Similarly, Steemit users are vying for upvotes, but this is because engagement and attention lead to actual financial reward. Steemit content creators are paid via members of the social platform and not from adverts. Utilizing cryptocurrency, Steemit users upvote and pay out a fraction of 'Steem' if they like content and want to support the author.

This innovative approach has given content creators a new way to connect with audiences via social media and get paid free of obstacles traditional mainstream social media networks have in place.

How does it all work?

Let's look a bit deeper into Steemit and review how their approach is different to other social platforms as well as the financial rewards on offer. Steemit, Inc. is a privately-held company based in New York City so behind this Blockchain platform is a private company, not just an unknown group of developers as is often the case for many Blockchain organizations. The platform is straightforward to use and Steemit.com is only one platform for blogs and social media content that sits on top of the Steem Blockchain. Steemit has adapted the social media model by creating an expanding social economy. This new type of economy or community rewards users for sharing their opinion and has been classed as an 'attention economy'. The entire Steem operation is founded on secure Blockchain software that runs on a network of computers. Core to the platform's offering is the currency Steem, which is a transferrable, freely moveable token that is similar to Bitcoin. The currency available comes in three different forms, the first being Steem, the central unit of account within the Steem Blockchain. All other tokens within the system form their value from the base value of Steem. Steem can be exchanged in any way that the holder decides, i.e. exchanged, sold or sought. It can then be converted to the two other options, namely Steem Power (SP) and Steem Dollars (SD). Users can also convert SP back into Steem, which is referred to as 'powering down'. Updating Steem into Steem Power is collectively known as 'powering up'. Here is where it gets a bit more complicated. Steem Power creates an incentive mechanism whereby holders register a long-term interest in a certain project and by having Steem Power, it increases an account's voting weight and consequently the ability to receive additional financial reward.

The final option is Steem Dollars (SD), which are linked to the US dollar. Here, Steemit promise to distribute one US dollar worth of Steem per SD to the token holder at some point in the future. Users are able to trade Steem Dollars with Steem, or alternatively, transfer them to other accounts for commerce or exchange. The goal here is to provide a channel to lend the community money and to effectively increase growth. The Steem Blockchain is consistently minting new Steem tokens and adding them to their community 'rewards pool'. Steem is then awarded to users for their contributions, which is rooted in the votes that their individual content receives. So, in a nutshell, if you create engaging valuable content, you receive financial rewards. If the content created earns money, 50 per cent is given to the user in Steem Dollars, which can be exchanged for actual cash right away if the owner wishes to receive this. The remaining 50 per cent is paid out in Steem Power and the Steem Power Units are kept in a vesting period, which is the period of time before shares in a stock option plan are unconditionally owned by the user.

Is this new approach really worth it?

We've gone through how Steemit actually functions and operates, but can it really work for brands looking to share content on the platform and make money from it? Well, that depends, as some users have had reasonable success while others have not. The main cause of frustration is that any content published effectively has a shelf life as long as a Tweet, if it is not upvoted into the trending section very quickly, and more can be achieved using established digital channels such as a blog site or social platforms with stronger monetization tools. For organizations that post on their social media brand communities (SMBCs) and already have a strong social following there may be a reluctance to join platforms like Steemit as this would mean time and effort to convince all of your followers to get on board the platform to further support you. Alternatively, if you are a smaller operation and willing to gamble on being an early adopter, willing to invest time and money in Steem Power, or you develop relationships with those holding SP, you could potentially leverage these positions to make money on your content. As with any social media platform channel, there are individuals and brands who are consistently leading the race whereas others despite best intentions are not at the level they wish to be. If your organization has pre-existing content for your offering that you can promote and share then it might be worth exploring this avenue further, while keeping expectations of success at a reasonable level. Before you decide to provide content it's worth considering a few aspects of your strategy, which are applicable to all social platforms.

First, remember that Steemit is basically a vast collection of smaller communities. Similar to Reddit, there are various content topics that are subdivided that you can tag. You can increase your chances of attracting views and being upvoted by learning how they are categorized. You can do this by researching previous content areas proven to be popular and then look at how you can add to these popular topics with your insight. Content types that do well not just on Steemit but other social channels too tend to include focused extensive articles delving into a subject matter or short pieces that provide quick overviews and often include humour. Before you begin to get involved with Steemit, it's worthwhile determining which aspects you will focus on to establish your content reputation.

Summary

The fundamental factor with Steemit is that anyone can use it and anyone can get paid without posting a single ad. Users are also rewarded for sharing or curating popular content. Curating involves voting on comments and post submissions and vote strength and curation rewards are influenced by the amount of Steem Power held by the voter. This might sound complicated but think back to the time when someone first explained social media to you and how easy it is to grasp now. Steemit is a perfect example of how new relationships between social media and cryptocurrency are developing, impacting the way social networks are managed and utilized, as now users can be free of censorship and payment restrictions. Steemit's use of Blockchain technology is undeniably innovative and useful for individuals and organizations, as there have long been calls within industry for a decentralized version of Reddit, where there are financial incentives for those who provide content and are duly rewarded for their skill and expertise. While Steemit's payment model is effective it is not without fault and payments to content creators are subject to volatile crypto market fluctuations, which can be really confusing.

Social platforms such as Steemit that are decentralized may not be, nor ever will be, as popular as the established juggernauts such as Facebook and LinkedIn, but imitation is the sincerest form of flattery and Steemit now has a lot more competition from networks providing a similar offering, such as E-chat, so there must be some merit to the approach. Blockchain projects are secure, sustainable, progressive and encourage quality content. They could be the social platform of choice for consumers in the future but for the time being, we will have to place them in the 'maybe' sub-category.

7

Digital Trust and Engagement Review

This book has sought to highlight the constructs that develop consumer online trust and in turn build reputation for brands using social media brand communities (SMBCs). Digital brand trust can be developed through brand SMBCs and is defined through core constructs, with an awareness of the importance of visuals, incentives and co-creation of social media value for consumers to develop brand trust through social media platforms. Various frameworks are proposed to further understand the trust constructs which provide a holistic view of how trust is perceived in a social media context. Having created initial trust with transactions, the focus then turns to continual trust and customer retention for brands. In order to sustain continual trust, brands must consistently provide 'value' to customers and the frameworks emphasize the need for brands to focus on these areas, adopting a customer focus plus a flexible and adaptable approach.

Engagement managerial implications

In providing a consumer trust and engagement framework, this book provides brands with an enhanced understanding of the 'engagement' concept which can assist organizations with developing consumer relationships and loyalty. In today's highly competitive digital environment, businesses are faced with the challenge of retaining customers who may display brand switching behaviours. Therefore, a brand's ability to measure and quantify continual trust against their organizational objectives and key performance indicators (KPIs) is expected to generate enhanced understanding of a target audience, objectives and its outcomes, including consumer-perceived brand trust and loyalty.

Since engagement is key to the continuation of a brand's social media presence, organizations should encourage active commentators and 'fans' of their SMBCs in such a way that leads not only to more commenting and liking, but to the development of relationships and influences purchase behaviour (e.g. value-focused content). Along with handling consumer user-generated content (UGC), brands should create their own content which adds value for consumers visiting the social media brand community and encourage them to engage in transactional behaviours. Furthermore, organizations should consistently monitor what motivates consumers to 'follow' or 'like' a community, the type of content they enjoy and what benefits they perceive in order to find ways to create added value for consumers to meet and exceed their expected benefits. All organizations should have the objective of increasing engagement with their customers through their social media activity. However, consumers' social media activity can vary in terms of their engagement with social media platforms, spending minutes or even hours of each day viewing content. Consumers' engagement levels with the SMBC vary due to their attitudes towards the brand, which is dependent on their motivations to become a member on social media. Some fans or followers may even post negative comments, all the while remaining members who continue to use the brand whereas some consumers join the platform to receive assistance, gain product knowledge and information, share their ideas and concerns or simply for entertainment.

Furthermore, consumers may decide to become fans as the community was recommended to them by other connections in their network, by way of a direct recommendation or even the influence of a retweet on Twitter or share on Facebook. These differing levels of engagement highlight that a brand's social media communities do not have the same impact for all consumers. Social media engagement provides a variety of potential connections for consumers as a result providing a variety of engagement options for consumers, which should result in highly engaged consumers forming positive relationships with the brand.

Value – Managerial implications

A number of factors may lead to a brand creating SMBCs, such as fast growth and popularity of social media, their viral nature, the competitors' presence on social media and the low-cost solutions offered by social media platforms. The organization's strategy and target audience may also be a factor. For example, if a brand's consumer target audience is comprised of a relatively young demographic, they may decide to have a strong social media presence. Or if an organization sells technological products, they may feel that the product capabilities are best displayed using social media. Given these factors, it could be argued that if a company creates an SMBC, the platform has to be appropriate and represent the brand's products or strategy. For example, a Facebook brand community would be more appropriate for a brand that desires full interactive communication with its target audience whereas a Twitter feed can spread short, informational messages. Brands that have visualized messages such as product demonstrations are more likely to prefer a YouTube channel. However, most organizations prefer a combination of several SMBCs, utilizing each one according to the needs of their social media strategy or target audience. In utilizing the daily and direct communication offered by social media communities, companies are able to keep prospects and customers close to the brand and are provided with the opportunity of turning them into a fan and a loyal customer, thereby increasing sales potential for the organization. Further sales strategies could also include traditional methods such as discounts, offers and competitions to increase sales.

Due to a number of operational factors such as low cost, demographic shifts, technological developments and consumer preference, the time and resources that brands are investing into social media activity is growing. As Neal Schaffer, author, CEO & Principal Social Media Strategy Consultant at Maximize Your Social, suggested in 2019

'With organic social media for brands slowly trending towards zero across all social media platforms, businesses in 2019 will have to focus on two things to be able to continue to be seen in the newsfeed of their fans and target audience: 1. Engage and build relationships with influencers and invest in a comprehensive and long-term influencer relations program, and 2. Invest exponentially more in newer content mediums such as stories and live streaming, as well as more traditional visual content mediums such as photo and video. Brands need to move from a text-first approach to a visual-first mentality when communicating, and similar to how every business became a media company with the advent of social media, they now must transform themselves into a visual magazine if not a television station in order to continue to be heard by the audience that matters to them.'

This implies that brands are becoming increasingly focused on establishing a presence within social media, creating value for consumers and developing long-term relationships. Given these issues and the high potential for marketing and creating trust through social media, a key challenge for brands is how to take full advantage of social media and find ways in which it can contribute to organizational objectives and support communications and marketing strategies.

Organizations fundamentally need a clear understanding of the purpose of social media for their business, whether a substitute or a supplementary tool to the rest of their communication activities. Possible synergies of social media with other online and offline actions should be carefully examined and systematically managed. Such synergies can for instance increase a brand's website or store visits. Also, the development of key performance indicators (KPIs) would provide organizations with the ability to analyse and review the performance of their social media activity. Since engagement is a key benefit for a brand's social media presence, firms should encourage active commentators and 'likers' in their pages in such a way that leads not only to more commenting and liking, but also to purchase behaviour.

One of the first consequences of having a highly involved consumer base is converting consumers to 'fans'. Rather than looking for short-term engagements that spike then fade away, by asking consumers to share experiences, fans help shape the evolution of the brand and can strengthen their connection, thereby creating brand enthusiasm and building consumer trust and loyalty in the long term for businesses and expanding their customer base. By shaping content to focus on the experience for consumers when they visit or become part of a SMBC, brands can engage with customers and potential customers on a large scale, driving advocacy and e-WOM.

If businesses strive to engage with new and existing customers to create and sustain trust then they are required to incorporate a staged process in order to acquire and retain consumers using SMBCs. Brands would be wise to review the proposed stages within the process to develop engaging strategies which align with the organization's social media and organizational objectives, as well as consumer preferences. The engagement process can then be used as a practical tool to enable organizations to establish a comprehensive variety of strategic content to demonstrate the brand's commitment to encouraging consumer trust. The process could also be used as a framework to review the strengths and weaknesses of social media campaigns. Evaluating social media engagement campaigns not only indicates whether or not they have met their objectives, but could also generate fresh ideas and new opportunities.

Reputation – Managerial implications

The challenge of transparency takes various forms in brand social media communities. The future of brand management may lie in systematic brand protection and relatively passive reputation management rather than active brand building. Alternatively, organizations may decide to adopt a more proactive strategy, where knowledgeable staff monitor the brand social media communities. However, in order to be successful, staff must be able to empathize with bloggers and posters and also create authentic engaging content and build 'buzz'. Other methods of maintaining transparency online include creating organizational policies, guidelines and practices for social media in general, as well as for specific forms of communication – organizational blogging, for instance. However, when adopting social media as a part of their daily processes, organizations should be mindful of the associated risks, emphasizing that formal rules and systems need to be created for employees to use in responding to social-media posts. Nevertheless, too much control may result in inauthentic brand communication and lead to a sense of alienation and resistance among staff. A balance between control and trust is therefore likely to be a crucial management challenge for any organization.

E-WOM managerial implications

One of the worst things you can do when someone has left a negative post on your SMBC is to delete it. Deleting comments can make it look like you just don't agree, don't care, or are trying to hide something. There are of course exceptions to this rule. If an individual posts abuse or inappropriate content (e.g. spam) then you could decide to delete and block them. A clear strategy is required to handle and respond to such comments. Indeed, even those companies who do respond to negative comments do not always adopt explicit strategies that transform those comments into useful opportunities to create and develop trust. Handling these instances poorly may result in further negative e-WOM among consumers. Consequently, a major challenge for businesses is to develop appropriate response strategies to negative word of mouth otherwise their SMBC may have negative impacts on a firm's brand image and sales. Brands should be aware of the high likelihood that consumers visit a social media community primarily for its supply of unique, trustworthy information, making the communication platforms avenues with enormous potential to spread influence. Better knowledge of the SMBC users is therefore required for organizations to fully utilize the commercial potential of social media. One of the main benefits of e-WOM for businesses is the generation of positive social media posts, which is a highly desirable result. To achieve this, organizations are presented with the important challenge of being capable of processing and managing e-WOM in a manner that generates messages and content favourable to new and existing customers. As a result, social media platforms that are useful and easy to use should be employed.

Moreover, organizations should promote the possibility of linking and sharing the information created by an integration of links from additional social networks – for instance, comments from a company blog that can also be shared on Twitter, Facebook, etc. The objective of brands wishing to benefit from the effects of social media engagement should focus on platforms that tend to the informational needs of their target audience and have influential users. Techniques to incentivize the participation of prescribers within a social network could also be used. Monitoring the distinct users of social communities through the use of key words, number of visits to the comment sections, number of comments, number of videos created, etc. is also a consideration. Once identified, special attention may be given to them in order to convince them of the positive qualities of promoting the brand's products or services. However, new and experienced users are equally likely to share marketing messages with other consumers as e-WOM's behaviour emerges from the basic human needs to be useful and to give advice. Therefore, brands should not underestimate the enormous potential for recommendation about products, held not only by individuals who are considered key influencers, but also by the majority of consumers.

SMBC research approach

Social constructionist research into social media is an evolving area and a main task for brands conducting consumer trust research is to investigate the different constructions and perceptions people place upon their individual experience when engaging with an SMBC. As social media is a dynamic platform, social constructionist research can be utilized in order to develop a deeper understanding of online engagement. When carrying out research, it is important your brand considers multiple viewpoints for the SMBC approach and content, which is why key informants and consumer insight must be considered to provide a holistic view of how digital trust can be achieved for brands. By adopting a multiple voices approach and combining the findings, brands are then potentially provided with a rich picture of social media engagement and consumer trust formation. The netnography approach has a number of advantages, particularly the rich data available from the SMBCs as well as the relatively easy access to the data. However, the sheer volume of information can be off-putting for some brands, which may deter them from using this method. Nevertheless, an approach where central and less central texts are identified prior to the netnography commencement can help keep the data recording and analysis more manageable for researchers with time and resource constraints.

Implications and application: Consumer trust

This book has shown that consumers identify with a number of brand activities that create and sustain consumer trust. The consumer trust roadmap may allow businesses to identify strengths, weaknesses and opportunities in relation to the potential for developing relationships with consumers. The roadmap may also be used as a strategic social media content planning tool to evaluate and establish competitive positioning within sectors as a method of identifying and developing competitiveness. Adopting a strategic plan to building initial trust and sustaining continual trust in this manner could also aid industry researchers, in order to better understand online purchasing behaviour. Taking a holistic view on consumer trust for social media, brand communities can assist brands with consumer acquisition and retention. However, the strength of this approach is that it provides organizations with a planning tool that facilitates the development of long-lasting, trusting relationships with consumers.

REFERENCES

Adidas-group.com (2017) 'Annual Report, 2017' viewed 14 December 2018

Aggarwal, Pankaj. (2004). 'The Effects of Brand Relationship Norms on Consumer Attitudes and Behavior', *Journal of Consumer Research*, 31. 10.1086/383426.

Ashworth, C.J. (2008). 'Organizational development, continuity and success in UK SME fashion e-retailing: A critical case approach', MMU PhD thesis.

Biddyco.com (2017) 'Peel Advertising case study', viewed 4 October 2018, https://biddyco.com/peel-case-study/

Brodie, R.J., Hollebeek, L.D., Juric, B. and Ilic, A. (2011). 'Customer Engagement: Conceptual Domain, Fundamental Propositions, and Implications for Research', *Journal of Service Research*, 14(3), 252–271.

CIO.com- Hassell, J (2016). 'What is blockchain and how does it work?', viewed 17 May 2018, https://www.cio.com/article/3055847/what-is-blockchain-and-how-does-it-work.html

Collective Bias (2018). URL: https://www.collectivebias.com/blog/celebrity-star-power-influences-men-and-women-differently

Custodio, Nik, https://www.medium.com/free-code-camp/explain-bitcoin-like-im-five-73b4257ac833

DigitalMarketingInstitute.com (2017) 'How Influencer Marketing Can Pump Up Your Content Strategy', viewed 9 July 2018, https://digitalmarketinginstitute.com/en-gb/blog/2017-10-10-how-influencer-marketing-can-pump-up-your-content-strategy

Drucker, P.F. (1999). *Management Challenges for the 21st Century*, HarperBusiness, New York.

Edelman (2018). URL: https://www.edelman.com/research/trust-barometer-brands-social-media

European Central Bank (2012) 'Virtual Currency Schemes' viewed February 2018, https://www.ecb.europa.eu/pub/pdf/other/virtualcurrencyschemes201210en.pdf

Facebook.com/Business (2019) 'Clinique France success', viewed 18 2019, https://www.facebook.com/business/success/clinique-france

https://marketingland.com/heigl-vs-duane-reade-lesson-tweet-79926

Facebook Newsroom (2018) 'The Hunt for False News' viewed 5 December 2018, https://newsroom.fb.com/news/2018/10/inside-feed-hunt-false-news-october-2018/

Forbes (2017). URL: https://www.forbes.com/sites/yec/2017/07/13/how-to-incorporate-video-into-your-social-media-strategy/#4e5e04457f2e

Feng, Mai, Zhe Shan, Qing Bai, Xin (Shane) Wang and Roger H.L. Chiang (2018). 'How Does Social Media Impact Bitcoin Value? A Test of the Silent Majority Hypothesis', pp. 9–52.

Google.com (2019) 'Ten things we know to be true' viewed 3 August 2019, https://www.google.com/intl/en/about/philosophy.html

Granovetter, Mark S. (1973). 'The Strength of Weak Ties', *American Journal of Sociology* 78(6):1360–80.

Granovetter, Mark S. (1985). 'Economic Action and Social Structure: The Problem of Embeddedness', *American Journal of Sociology*, 91: 481–510.

Gummesson, E. (2001). 'Are current research approaches in marketing leading us astray?' *Marketing Theory*, 1(3), 27–48

Gummesson, E. (2005). 'Qualitative research in marketing', *European Journal of Marketing*, Vol. 39 No. 3/4, pp. 309-327. https://doi.org/10.1108/03090560510581791

Habibi, M.R., Laroche, M. and Richard, M.-O. (2014). 'Brand communities based in social media: How unique are they? Evidence from two exemplary brand communities', *International Journal of Information Management*, 34(2), 123–132.

Hollebeek, L.D. (2011). 'Demystifying customer brand engagement: Exploring the loyalty nexus', *Journal of Marketing Management*, Vol. 27 Nos. 7–8, pp. 785–807.

Hootsuite, *We Are Social* (2019). 'The Global State of Digital in 2019 Report' viewed 2 August 2019, https://hootsuite.com/pages/digital-in-2019

Kozinets, R.V. (2002). 'The Field behind the Screen: Using Netnography for Marketing Research in Online Communities', *Journal of Marketing Research*, Vol. XXXIX, pp.61–72.

Kulms, P. and Kopp, S. (2018). 'A social cognition perspective on human-computer trust: The effect of perceived warmth and competence on trust in decision-making with computers', *Frontiers in Digital Humanities*, 5.

Market Track (2017). URL: https://blog.markettrack.com/shopper-survey.

Marketingweek.com (2018) 'Social connections: Weaving social media into the customer journey' viewed 25 June 2018, https://www.marketingweek.com/social-media-customer-journey/

Miles, M.B. and Huberman, A.M. (2nd edn, 1994). *Qualitative Data Analysis: An Expanded Source Book*, Sage, Newbury Park, CA.

Muniz, A.M. and O'Guinn, T.C. (2001). 'Brand Community', *Journal of Consumer Research*, 2001; 27(4), 412–432. Viewed August 2018 via Google Scholar.

Nakamoto. S. (2008). *Bitcoin: A Peer-to-Peer Electronic Cash System*. Available online: https://bitcoin.org/bitcoin.pdf

Noort, G. van and Willemsen, L. (2011). 'Online Damage Control: The Effects of Proactive Versus Reactive Webcare Interventions in Consumer-generated and Brand-generated Platforms'

Popper, N. (2015). *Digital Gold – Bitcoin and the Inside Story of the Misfits and Millionaires Trying to Reinvent Money*. Harper, New York.

'Proactive Versus Reactive Webcare Interventions in Consumer-generated and Brand-generated Platforms', *Journal of Interactive Marketing* (26), 131–140.

PWC: 'Global Consumer Insights Survey 2018: Whom do consumers really trust?' URL: https://www.pwc.com/gx/en/retail-consumer/assets/consumer-trust-global-consumer-insights-survey.pdf

Sashi, C.M. (2012). 'Customer engagement, buyer–seller relationships, and social media', *Management Decision*, Vol. 50, No. 2, pp. 253–272.

Sprout Social (2018). URL: https://sproutsocial.com/insights/data/q2-2017/

Statistica.com (2018). URL: https://www.statista.com/topics/2057/brands-on-social-media/

Taylor, D. G., Strutton, D & Thompson, K. (2012). 'Self-Enhancement as a Motivation for Sharing Online Advertising.' Journal of Interactive Advertising 12:13-28.

Urquhart, C. and Vaast, E. (2012). 'Building Social Media Theory from Case Studies: A New Frontier for IS Research' in: 33rd International Conference on Information Systems, Orlando, USA.

Vargo, S.L. and Lusch, R.F. (2004). 'Evolving to a New Dominant Logic for Marketing', *Journal of Marketing*, 68(1), 1–17.

Verge.com (2017) 'Steam no longer accepting bitcoin due to "high fees and volatility"', viewed 4 October 2018, https://www.theverge.com/2017/12/6/16743220/valve-steam-bitcoin-game-store-payment-method-crypto-volatility

World Economic Forum (2016) 'The Impact of Digital Content: Opportunities and Risks of Creating and Sharing Information Online', viewed 22 February 2017, http://www3.weforum.org/docs/GAC16/Social_Media_Impact_Digital.pdf

Zinnbauer, M. and Honer, T. (2011). 'How Brands Can Create Social Currency – a Framework for Managing Brands in a New Era', *Marketing Review*, St. Gallen 28: 50–55.

BIBLIOGRAPHY

Alvesson, M. & Skoldberg, K. (2000). *Reflexive Methodology: New Vistas for Qualitative Research*. London: Sage.

Banks, M. (2007). *Using Visual Data in Qualitative Research*. London: Sage.2

Bryman, A. and Bell, E. (2004). *Business Research Methods*, Oxford: Oxford University Press.

Burr, V. (1995). '*An Introduction to Social Constructionism*. London: Routledge.4

Cassell, C.M. & Symon, G. (1994). *Qualitative Methods in Organizational Research*. London: Sage

Covey, Stephen (1989). *The 7 Habits of Highly Effective People*, New York: Free Press.

Davies, D., & Dodd, J. (2002). 'Qualitative research and the question of rigor'. *Qualitative Health research*, 12(2), 279–289.

Denzin, N. & Lincoln, Y. (2003), 'The Discipline and Practice of Qualitative Research', in Denzin, N. & Lincoln, Y. (eds.) *Collecting and Interpreting Qualitative Materials*, 2nd edn, SAGE Publications, Inc., California, pp. 1–45

Di Pietro, L & Pantano, E. (2012). 'An Empirical Investigation of Social Network Influence on Consumer Purchasing Decision: The Case of Facebook.' *Journal of Direct Data and Digital Marketing Practice* 14: 18–29.

Easterby-Smith, M., Golden-Biddle, K., and Locke, K. (2008) 'Working with pluralism: determining quality in qualitative research.' *Organizational Research Methods*, 11(3): 419–429.

Fast Company-Web URL: https://www.fastcompany.com/1682625/the-myth-of-marketing-how-research-reaches-for-the-heart-but-only-connects-with-the-head

Fournier, S, & Avery, J (2011). 'The uninvited brand,' *Business Horizons*, 54(3), 193–207.

Gillham, B (2000). *Case Study Research Methods*. London: Continuum.

Gummesson, E. (2000). *Qualitative Methods in Management Research*. London: Sage

Hennig-Thurau, T., Hofacker, C. F., & Bloching, B. (2013). 'Marketing the pinball way: Understanding how social media change the generation of value for consumers and companies'. *Journal of Interactive Marketing*, 27(4), 237–241.

Jackson, S. (2009). *The Cult of Analytics: Driving Online Marketing Strategies Using Web Analytics*. Oxford, UK: Butterworth-Heinemann.

Kim, B., & Han, I. (2009). 'The role of trust belief and its antecedents in a community-driven knowledge environment'. *Journal of the American Society for Information Science and Technology*, 60(5), 1012–1026.

McKnight, D.H., Choudhury, & V., Kacmer, C., (2002). 'The impact of initial trust on intentions to transact with a web site: a trust building model'. *Journal of Strategic Information Systems* 11 (3), 297–323.

Van Praet, Douglas (2012). *Unconscious Branding: How Neuroscience Can Empower (and Inspire) Marketing*, New York: Palgrave MacMillan.

ACKNOWLEDGEMENTS

My father was made redundant from his job at 58 and took the brave decision to set up an online store. With my professional experience and background I was able to help build the website and develop the social platforms, but in a competitive market and with a lack of resources we needed to find ways to stand out from the competition. My father had formed a strong professional reputation within the arts and reprographics industry and many of his customers trusted him to always deliver quality products at a fair price and on time. So the challenge was transferring the trusting characteristics and values that my father stood for and promoting them digitally. The psychology of how trust is developed and can be easily lost has always fascinated me and inspired me to begin a doctorate in the area, learning more about consumer engagement to help with the promotion of my father's business. My father has since retired but the business was extremely successful for the time it was in operation. A large part of this I'm convinced was due to how we promoted our brand values online in that we were a trustworthy organization that truly cared about our customers.

I was then highly motivated to share my research findings and strategies with other similar small businesses to help them compete in tough environments, so the idea for this book was a natural platform to share my findings. My parents Richard and Colette have always been an inspiration to me and I can't thank them enough for all the support they have given me over the years. The support from the families; Turner, Amos, Gordon, Hepburn, Cameron and Nisbett, has also meant the world to me.

Thank you to all the wonderful academics who have supported me both professionally and academically over the years at Liverpool

John Moores University, Manchester Metropolitan University, and the University of Edinburgh. A special thank you to my former PhD supervisor Dr Catherine Ashworth who was a source of constant support and encouragement during my time as a student.

Finally, thank you also to my beautiful wife Donna and daughter Charlotte; you are my world and inspire me every single day.

INDEX